1776 FAITH

THE CHRISTIAN WORLDVIEW OF THE SIGNERS OF THE DECLARATION OF INDEPENDENCE

by

Phil Webster

Copyright © 2009 by Phil Webster

1776 Faith
The Christian Worldview of the Signers of
the Declaration of Independence
by Phil Webster

Printed in the United States of America

ISBN 9781615794157

All rights reserved solely by the author. The author guarantees all contents are original and do not infringe upon the legal rights of any other person or work. No part of this book may be reproduced in any form without the permission of the author. The views expressed in this book are not necessarily those of the publisher.

Unless otherwise indicated, Bible quotations are taken from The New International Version of the Bible. Copyright © 1973, 1978, 1984 by the International Bible Society.

www.xulonpress.com

Dedicated to my loving mother

Nanetta Reddish Webster Phillips

A woman who has invested in people;
who taught me a lot about trusting the Lord,
having common sense
and a good sense of humor.

"…a woman who fears the Lord, she shall be praised."
Proverbs 31:30b

I would like to thank my wife Jean who put up with the many hours of this project and allowed me to use her family's drawing on the front cover. It is the draft drawing of "The Continentals" by Frank Blackwell Mayer, 1875. Thanks go out to my children Carolyn, Joseph, Daniel and Elizabeth who have to put up with John Jay in the house. Thanks go out to the many people who have encouraged me through this project: Ron Cheadle and the people of Reliance E. Free Church in Dover, Rev. Jason Shelton and the people of Providence Presbyterian Church in Salisbury, Maryland. Thanks also to my niece Kate Lilley (who made a coat of the American Revolutionary period) and to the librarians at Salisbury University and Wicomico County Free Library. Encouragers such as Bonnie and Luis Luna, Ted Cogswell and Matt Smith have helped me keep focused.

1776 Faith Index

Introduction xiii
   Introduction- The Great Plan of Providence xiii
   Take the Founders' Challenge xv
   Author's Notes xvii

I. The Signers of the Declaration of Independence: 19
   The Christian Aspects of the Declaration of Independence 21
      Georgia: Button Gwinnett, Lyman Hall, George Walton
      South Carolina: Thomas Heyward, Jr., Thomas Lynch, Jr.,
         Edward Rutledge, Arthur Middleton
      North Carolina: Joseph Hewes, John Penn, William
         Hooper
      Virginia: George Wythe, Richard Henry Lee, Thomas
         Nelson, Jr., Francis Lightfoot Lee, Benjamin Harrison,
         Carter Braxton, Thomas Jefferson
      Maryland: Samuel Chase, William Paca, Charles Carroll,
         Thomas Stone
      Delaware: Caesar Rodney, Thomas McKean, George Read
      Pennsylvania: Benjamin Franklin, Benjamin Rush, George
         Clymer, John Morton, George Ross, James Wilson,
         James Smith, Robert Morris
      New Jersey: Abraham Clark, John Hart, Francis
         Hopkinson, Richard Stockton, John Witherspoon
      New York: Francis Lewis, Philip Livingston, William
         Floyd, Lewis Morris

Massachusetts: Samuel Adams, John Adams, Robert Treat Paine, Elbridge Gerry, John Hancock
Rhode Island: Stephen Hopkins, William Ellery
Connecticut: Roger Sherman, Samuel Huntington, William Williams, Oliver Wolcott
New Hampshire: Josiah Bartlett, William Whipple, Matthew Thornton

Additional Insights into the Following Founders: George Wythe, Benjamin Franklin, Benjamin Rush, Roger Sherman, John Adams and Samuel Adams..................113

II. Other Christian Founders
    George Washington..................128
    Patrick Henry..................135
    John Dickinson..................139
    Alexander Hamilton..................141
    John Jay..................145
    Elias Boudinot..................158

III. Objection! What about Thomas Paine? 162
    In America- Christian Worldview
    In France- Atheistic Worldview
    After Age of Reason-not welcome in the United States

IV. Supposed "Separation of Church and State..................171
    Freedom of religion, not freedom from religion..................173
    Northwest Ordinance and "Separation"..................172
    Northwest Ordinance specifics..................172

V. What About Jefferson? 174
VI Days of Prayer 180
VII. State Constitutions..................199

VIII. God's Providential Care in the War for Independence........206
    Evacuation of Long Island..................206
    Trenton and the Crossing of the Delaware..................209

Defeat of Burgoyne at Saratoga 209
Discovery of Benedict Arnold's treason 211
Retreat from Cowpens 212
Yorktown 213

IX. The Great Awakening 214
    The Schooling of the Founders
    10 sons of Ministers

X. Music of the American Revolution Era 217

XI. Christian Colleges: Yale, Harvard, Princeton, King's
    (Columbia), University of Pennsylvania and
    William Mary 225

XII. Bibliography 229

XIII. Picture Credits 235

Introduction

"A proper history of the United States would have much to recommend it: in some aspects it would be singular, or unlike all others; it would develop the great plan of Providence, for causing this extensive part of our world to be discovered, and these 'uttermost parts of the earth' to be gradually filled with civilized and Christian people and nations. The means or second causes by which this great plan has long been and still is accomplishing, are materials for history, of which the writer ought well to know the use and bearings and proper places. In my opinion, the historian, in the course of the work, is never to lose sight of that great plan."
John Jay to Rev. Dr. Jedediah Morse;
August 16, 1809

Following John Jay's advice, **a proper history of the United States would develop the great plan of Providence.** The first Chief Justice of the United States has charged writers of the history of the beginning of our country to **never lose sight of that great plan.** This book is an attempt to help the present generation rediscover the Christian heritage of our country. This is not an exhaustive treatise- it is a sampler. Hopefully the reader will do some digging on his/her own. Hopefully a lot of lights will be turned on across the nation. Many will ask: "Why has this been hidden?"

God has done something very special in human history through our nation. However, the direction of the nation in many ways is going against God. There are some positive things going on but we definitely have some major problems. We have aborted more babies in the United States than the current population of Canada. Also, do we have the sins of Sodom among us?

The all powerful hand of God is at work also- not just in our nation but around the world. Jesus Christ will set up His kingdom someday. God may do something totally unbelievable in our nation- He has done it before. Who would have thought that the Soviet Union would crumble 30 years ago?

In kind, loving ways share this book and shine the light of Christ. May the God of our fathers be real and living in the hearts of this generation!

Take the Founders' Challenge

There is a large debate in our society about whether God has a place in public in our society. The research for the debate needs to start on what the Founders of the country intended for the government. The best way to research them is to read the primary documents for themselves.

Many Americans depend on their information about the Founders from school textbooks and from television documentaries. What if the textbook editors have a strong bias against God? What if the television documentary you are watching has given you only a portion and not the whole picture on where these men stood about God? What if a whole generation or more has bought the lie of "separation of church and state" without ever reading the First Amendment by itself? There are a lot of questions that need to be raised on the subject.

While reading the writings of John Jay, I noticed that I was finding buried treasure. Not only was there great treasure with Jay; I found that there were veins of gold running to other people. After seeing so many Founders with deep Christian values, I started on some others in depth. I came across <u>The Letters of the Delegates of the Continental Congress.</u> It is a compilation of the public and private letters that delegates of the Continental Congress wrote from 1774 to 1789. I took notes in notebooks and then color coded them for each state and compiled each state and then each signer. I wanted to see where these gentlemen stood on the issue of whether God is honored or just barely allowed or hated. My question was answered through reading their writings. I would say that at least 54 of the 56 signers would be convicted of having a Christian worldview if such a thing were a crime. In my research, the other two have been hard to find much written at all as to make a good decision.

Reading their writings gave me the answer but it was confirmed at Carpenters' Hall. When you take your first step in the building, look at the floor. You have to walk over the words "**Honor God**". Those men had to walk over that. My answer was confirmed: Honor God would be the answer instead of just barely allowing God or hating God.

Author's Notes

The scope of this book is to focus on the period of the American Revolution, in order to see if the Founders of that period had a Christian, deistic or atheistic worldview. This book hopefully presents that there is another side than what is portrayed in most textbooks.

Please take the time to get quality portraits of the Founders and their wives when they were in their prime of life (not when they were old). Look closely at these men and women- they were real.

Many detractors will say that I cannot spell very well. As a Webster, I would take umbrage at such an accusation. The spellings are from the original writers so you the reader could get a sense of word usage of the time period. It is a vivid reminder of why Noah Webster went to such effort to compile the dictionary for American usage.

The writers of the Bible were imperfect people that God used. The Founders were imperfect but God used them. This writer humbly submits this book knowing that he also is a sinner and capable of error. I ask the same openness of the reader to see that there just might be a case to be made for the existence of God, the truthfulness of the Bible and the resurrection of Jesus Christ (check out Josh McDowell's book <u>Evidence That Demands a Verdict</u>). The God of history and of nations may have had a place for our nation. I was not at George Washington's first inauguration but I can just imagine that he had the Bible open at Deuteronomy 28 and 29 where it talks about the blessings and curses on a nation. If the Bible is right, if the resurrection really happened and if the United States really did have a Christian history, we stand on Mount Ebal. May God turn us around and make us once more a nation that follows Him. Please pray for our schools and our colleges and universities to once again have godly men and women teach.

    Psalm 11:3 "If the foundations are destroyed, what can the righteous do?"
    John 8:32 "And you shall know the truth and the truth will make you free."

The Signers of the Declaration of Independence

The Christian Aspects of the Declaration of Independence

Y ou may be shocked at the audacity of someone discussing the Christian aspects of the Declaration of Independence. Read the document for itself and test to see if it indeed has Christian elements. It is noted with sadness that some activist judges (in concert with the anti-God Gestapo) have ruled that the Declaration of Independence cannot be displayed in public schools for the very reason that it talks about God. Let's look at the text.

The focus here will be upon the first and last paragraphs of the Declaration. The middle portions deal with specific grievances that our country had with England. There are five references to God in the Declaration.

- the laws of Nature and of <u>Nature's God</u>
- We hold these truths to be self-evident, that all men are <u>created</u> equal
- that they are <u>endowed by their Creator</u> with certain unalienable rights
- appealing to <u>the Supreme Judge of the World</u>
- with <u>a firm reliance on the protection of Divine Providence</u>, we mutually pledge to each other our Lives, our Fortune and our Sacred Honor.

Take note that at the beginning of the last paragraph, it says: "We therefore the Representatives of the United States of America, in Congress Assembled, appealing to the Supreme Judge of the World..."No self-respecting atheist would sign such a document. Neither would a deist sign such a document saying "with a firm reliance on Divine Providence." Providence means God taking care of us in the here and now. Deists believe that God created the world and left it alone.

These men signed onto the Christian worldview contained in the document. Their signature is enough to convict them of a Christian worldview. However, let us examine their individual writings.

Button Gwinnett

In order to start examining the Christian faith of the signers of the Declaration we will go through a methodical look at each of the 56 signers. Let us start with Georgia. As the study begins, it is good to keep in mind how the Bible portrays people: all were sinners except one- Jesus Christ. Guess what? Our Founders were also sinners. Just like Abraham, Moses, Peter, Thomas, etc., our Founders made mistakes. However, they made noble contributions as well.

The first man to examine from Georgia is Button Gwinnett. His valid signature is worth at least $110,000 to $190,000. Georgia does not have the quantity of writings of other Founders. Their state was controlled by the British for a time during the War for Independence. Most assuredly, some documents were taken or burned. Button Gwinnett was a descendant of a Cromwell official. He became president of the state in May, 1776. There was a power dispute (with Colonel McIntosh) over who would lead the army. As president of the state, Gwinnett thought he should. The resulting duel led to Gwinnett's death on May 16, 1777.

As stated earlier, we don't know all the details of Mr. Gwinnett. The state constitution (over which he presided) stated that a person had to be a Protestant to hold office. Since he presided over the proceedings, it is safe to assume that he was not only a Christian but specifically a Protestant.

Button was baptized on April 10, 1735 at Down Hatherby, Gloucester, England. His father, Rev. Samuel Gwinnett was an Anglican minister. Button's older brother (another Rev. Samuel Gwinnett) was also an Anglican minister. Gwinnett was reticent to go as far as favor independence from England. Both his father and brother served as ministers in the Church of England, He also had a younger brother serving as an officer in the King's army.

> "Whereas in the present alarming situation of this State, it is absolutely necessary to do every thing in our Power to prevent any Intelligence, or Supplies being carried to our Enemies...

Given under my hand and Seal at Savannah, the fifth day of March, one thousand seven hundred and seventy seven
Button Gwinnett
God Save the Congress"
Button Gwinnett, March 5, 1777

Lyman Hall

Lyman Hall was a transplanted New England Puritan who moved to Georgia in 1752. He studied for the ministry but later changed and became a doctor instead. Does that mean he gave up his faith in Christ? You can serve God as a doctor, lawyer and I even have heard of at least one case of a carpenter.

He married Abigail Burr (a relative of Jonathan Edwards) who died at the age of 24. He remarried Mary Osborn and moved to South Carolina in 1752. About 40 New England families accompanied him in his move. These New Englanders brought with them the Puritan faith. Hall's property in Sunbury and Savannah was destroyed by the British and he had to move his family back to Connecticut. He returned to Georgia in 1782 and in the next year he was appointed governor.

The Tory Governor of Georgia who was ousted by American patriots, accused Lyman Hall and his followers as being "chiefly descendants of the Puritan sect," who followed "a strong tincture of Republican or Oliverian [Oliver Cromwell] principles."

Here is a quote from Mr. Hall while he served as governor of the state of Georgia on July 8, 1783:

> "In addition, therefore to wholesome laws restraining vice, every encouragement ought to be given to introduce religion, and learned clergy to perform divine worship in honor of God, and to cultivate principles of religion and virtue among our citizens. For this purpose it will be your wisdom to lay an early foundation for endowing seminaries of learning; nor can you, I conceive lay a better than by a grant of a sufficient tract of land, that may, as in other governments, hereafter, by lease or otherwise, raise a revenue sufficient to support such valuable institutions."

Consider the following from his tombstone: "But reader, above all, know from this inscription that he left this probatory state as a true Christian and an honest man."

George Walton

George Walton was born west of Richmond, Virginia in a town named Farmville. He was orphaned at an early age. His guardian apprenticed him to be a carpenter. His master did not appreciate his hunger for reading and learning, as he used torch-wood for light at night to study. When he finished his apprenticeship at age twenty, he moved from Virginia to Georgia.

Walton fell in with Lyman Hall and others of the Patriot cause. He was chosen as a delegate to the Continental Congress in 1776 and voted for independence. He stayed in Congress until 1778 when he returned to Georgia to help defend his state. Walton commanded a regiment with the rank of colonel. In the battle of Savannah, he was wounded in the thigh and taken prisoner.

Remember that the Georgia Constitution of 1777 said that all representatives not only had to be Christian but specifically Protestant. George Walton signed the Declaration of Independence and later became Chief Justice of Georgia.

George Walton, along with J.J. Zubly and N. W. Jones wrote the following as representatives of Georgia from the Continental Congress on July 25, 1775 as they talked about a day of prayer on June 19th and 20th: "To be observed as such, both days have been observed with a becoming solemnity; and we humbly hope many earnest prayers have been presented to the Father of Mercies on that day, through this extensive continent, and that He has heard the cries of the destitute, and will not despise their prayers."

George Walton was in the Provincial Congress of Georgia when they voted to pay a chaplain in the troops of Georgia (Later went up from $20 a month to $33 a month).

<u>(Journal of Provincial Congress, July 13, 1775) George Walton in attendance</u>

> "...Georgia, being persuaded that the salvation of the rights and liberties of America depend, under God, on the firm union of the inhabitants in its vigorous prosecution of the measures necessary for its safety,"

George Walton to his wife Dorothy, (Jan. 4, 1779)

"God bless you my dear, and remember that you are sincerely loved by a man who wishes to make honor and reputation the rule of his actions."

Edward Rutledge

Edward Rutledge's father came from Ireland to South Carolina as a doctor. Edward studied law by going to the Temple in London. When he returned in 1772 he was admitted to the bar to practice law. Although he was only 25 years old, he was elected as a delegate to the Continental Congress. In 1780, Rutledge was back in South Carolina heading a corps of artillery, and was taken prisoner by the British. He was exchanged a year later. In 1794 he was a senator and in 1798 elected governor. He died of a severe cold while in office in 1800.

Edward Rutledge to Robert R. Livingston, Aug. 19, 1776

"...I am much pleased with the Spirit of your convention. God grant they may receive the Blessings of Liberty, & by a wise government fix those Blessings upon a strong & lasting foundation."

Edward Rutledge to George Washington, Sept. 11, 1776

"Our Reliance continues therefore to be (under God) on your wisdom & fortitude & that of your Forces...God bless you my dear Sir."

Edward Rutledge to Ralph Izard (December 8, 1775) II, 463.

"This session may determine the Fate, of a great Kingdom- unless the Parliament improve the opportunity now offered them, they may loose forever their American Colonies. May God grant them Wisdom to discover- and Virtue to pursue such measures- as may best tend to the Establishment of Peace, and Happiness."

Edward Rutledge to Ralph Izard (December 8, 1775) II, 463

"...Surely if the Administration had consulted their friends, the Bishops, they could have informed them, that Christian charity – however strongly enjoined in Holy Writ- has seldom, if ever, extended and indiscriminate cruelties committed against the Inhabitants of this Country- that I do not believe I shall ever forget- or forgive them; and so determined am I on being free that I will even quit my Native Country without a sigh- if the Genius of Liberty shall loose her Influence. That, however, I trust will never be the case... unless the Parliament improve the opportunity now offered them, they may loose forever their American Colonies. May God grant them Wisdom to discover- and Virtue to pursue such measures- as may tend to the Establishment of Peace and Happiness."

Thomas Heyward, Jr.

Thomas Heyward was a lawyer who studied at the Temple in London.

He was chosen as a delegate to the Continental Congress in 1775 and remained there until 1778 when he was appointed judge of the criminal and civil courts of South Carolina. In the spring of 1780 Judge Heyward was commander of a battalion when Charleston was besieged and conquered by the British. He and others were imprisoned at St. Augustine, Florida. When he was returned to Philadelphia, he fell overboard but kept himself alive by holding on to the rudder. Imagine what went through his mind when he got back on board. Odds are real good that Thomas gave a big thank you to Somebody.

Here is an excerpt from a letter he wrote to John Morgan on Sept. 4, 1776:

> "...May the God of Heaven protect our General and his Army in this great Day of Trial and Distress & may the virtuous Efforts of our brave Countrymen be crowned with deserved Success."

While a prisoner in St. Augustine, he celebrated Independence Day by changing the words of the British national anthem. Instead of "God save the King," his song was "God save the thirteen States." Below are stanzas one and five.

> God save the Thirteen States!
> Long rule the United States!
> God save our States!
> Make us victorious,
> Happy and glorious;
> No tyrants over us;
> God save our States!
>
> O Lord! Thy gifts in store,
> We pray on Congress pour,

To guide our States.
May union bless our land,
While we, with heart and hand,
Our mutual rights defend;
God save our States!

Thomas Lynch, Jr.

Although born and raised in South Carolina, Thomas Lynch was sent to Eaton College and Cambridge in England. He then studied law at the Temple in London. He returned to South Carolina in 1772 and soon married Elizabeth Shubrick. In 1775 he was commissioned a captain in the state militia.

His father became ill while serving at the Continental Congress. Thomas was elected to take his father's place. He took his seat in 1776, signed the Declaration and then tried to take his father home. When they reached Annapolis, Thomas' father died. Thomas' own health was bad and he was advised by doctors to go to southern Europe. He and his wife left on a voyage in 1779. The ship they traveled on was never heard from again. It is supposed that it sank.

Two letters from Lynch to George Washington show his Christian belief.

Jan. 16, 1776

> "In the state of things, I have, beside my Dependence on the Continuation of the Favour of Heaven, Trust in two supports alone, the one on your Vigourous Exertions, the other on the Weakness of our Enemies."

Dec. 8, 1775

> "Providence favours us everywhere, our success in every operation exceeds our most sanguine expectations and yet when God is ready to deliver our oppressors into our hands, that Men cannot be found willing to receive them, is truly surprising."

Arthur Middleton

Like the other signers from South Carolina, Arthur Middleton was born and raised in South Carolina but was educated in England. In 1763 he graduated from Cambridge and later traveled through Europe. That same year he married Mary Izzard and worked as a justice of the peace and delegate to the provincial assembly. In 1768, he and his wife went on a trip to England, France and Spain. They returned in 1773. Even though he had many reasons to promote British business, he went with the patriot cause. In 1776 he was elected by the Provincial Legislature to be a delegate to the Continental Congress. A large part of his estate was destroyed and he himself was a British prisoner for about one year.

Arthur Middleton to Edward Rutledge, Sept. 17, 1782

"...The allied states [other countries] now amount to Twenty, God grant an Encrease of them."

South Carolina Constitution, March 19, 1778; Article XXXVIII:

"That all persons and religious societies who acknowledge that there is one God, and a future state of rewards and punishments, and that God is publicly to be worshipped, shall be freely tolerated. The Christian Protestant religion shall be deemed, and is hereby constituted and declared to be, the established religion of this State. That all denominations of Christian Protestants in this State, demeaning themselves peaceably and faithfully, shall enjoy equal religious and civil privileges...[any society of Christians can form] each society so petitioning shall have agreed to and subscribed in a book the following five articles, (see p. 200)

William Hooper

Neither of the signers from North Carolina was born there. William Hooper was born in Boston, the son of a minister (Trinity Church). He graduated from Harvard with a law degree and then worked in the law office of James Otis (a powerful firebrand of independence). When he got his license to practice law, he moved from Massachusetts to North Carolina in 1767. In 1773 he represented Wilmington in the general assembly. He was elected to the Continental Congress in 1774 where he served until 1777. After the war he served as one of the judges of the federal court and died in 1790.

William Hooper to the North Carolina Convention, Nov. 14, 1776

> "We have this moment received Intelligence from the Jersies that 100 of Enemies Ships steering Southwerd, the Congress have thought proper to dispatch An express to you that you may hold yourselves in immediate readiness to oppose any attempts against your state, or to render assistance to your Neighbors…We are making every preparation to oppose any designs they may have against this place & with the blessing of God, I confide shall be able to disappoint them."

William Hooper to Joseph Hewes, Nov. 29, 1776

> "The people here are vastly comforted with 7 days of Rainy Weather which we have had as it must retard Gen. Howe's progress thro' the Jersies. Heaven they say fights for them, well that it does for they attempt nothing for themselves. If Salvation comes to them it is the superabundant unmerited grace of God which gives to Sinners infinitely more than they can ask or think."

William Hooper's Draft Resolve (June 7-12, 1775) I, 455-456

"Resolved that it be and hereby it is recommended to the Inhabitants of the united Colonies in America of all Denominations That Thursday the 20th of July next be set apart as a day of public humiliation fasting and prayer, that a total Abstinence from Servile labor and recreation be observed and all their religious assemblies Solomnly Convened to humble themselves before God under the heavy Judgments felt and threatened to confess our manifold Sins, to implore the forgiveness of Heaven, (that a sincere repentance & reformation may influence may influence our future conduct)..."

Joseph Hewes

Joseph Hewes was born in New Jersey in 1730 to Quaker parents. Keep the Quaker background in mind for a later quote. Joseph graduated from Princeton and worked as a merchant in Philadelphia. At the age of thirty he moved to North Carolina. He represented North Carolina from 1774 until his death in 1779.

<u>Joseph Hewes to Samuel Johnston, May 11, 1775</u>

> "...All the Quakers except a few of the old Rigid ones have taken up arms, there is not one company without several of these people in it, and I am told one or two of the companies are composed entirely of Quakers... New York has been Converted almost as instantaneously as St. Paul was of old, a Tory dare not open his mouth either in that Province or this. The Battle near Boston & the Act of Parliament for restraining the Trade of all the Colonies except New York & N. Carolina has wrought the conversion of New York. I wish to God it may have the same effect on our Province."

<u>Joseph Hewes to Samuel Johnston, Jan. 4, 1776</u>

> "The Congress at our request have agree to send two Clergymen to North Carolina to explain to the Highlanders and regulators the nature of the dispute between Great Britain and the Colonies, and left the appointment to us [N.C. delegates]. We applied to Mr. Elihu Spencer and Mr. Alexander McWhorter two eminent divines of the Presbyterian religion who have undertaken the service."

<u>Joseph Hewes to James Iredell (May 17,1776) IV, 26.</u>

> "This being a day of humiliation, fasting (or in Vulgar language Congress Sunday) I mean to steal as much time from my private devotions as will serve to acknowledge the

receipt of your agreeable favour of the 29th ultimo which has just reached me."

Joseph Hewes and Robert Smith to a London Mercantile Firm (July 31, 1775), I, p. 685

"...We do not want to be independent, we want no revolution, unless a change of Ministry, and measures would be deemed such; we are loyal subjects to our present most gracious Sovereign, in support of whose crown and dignity we would sacrifice our lives,...We say again, for the love of Heaven, the love of liberty...we conjure you to exert yourselves."

John Penn

John Penn's father died in Virginia when John was 18 years old. The sudden inheritance at such an early age almost ruined John. A relative, Edmund Pendleton, took him under his wing and helped direct his steps to studying and becoming a lawyer. In 1774, John moved to North Carolina. He was elected a member of the Continental Congress, starting in October 1775 until 1779.

John Penn to Thomas Person, Feb. 13, 1776

"For God sake my Good Sir encourage our People, animate them to dare even to die for their Country."

North Carolina Constitution 1776

Article XXXII(5) "That no person, who shall deny the being of God or the truth of the Protestant religion, or the divine authority of the Old or New Testaments, or who shall hold religious principles incompatible with the freedom and safety of the State, shall be capable of holding any office or place of trust or profit in the civil department within this State."

John Penn to John Jay; August 27, 1779

"If my prayers or wishes are of any consequence, you are restored to health long before this; pray Remember me to Sir James, Colo. Livingston, Mrs. Jay, and Lady Kitty and believe me to be with great truth, Your sincere Friend &c, J. **Penn**"

George Wythe

Many biographies or surveys of the signers overlook or minimize the life of George Wythe. This man taught Jefferson, Madison and others like John Marshall at William and Mary. One would do well to question what exactly George Wythe taught. He taught a lot from Blackstone. So what, who is Blackstone? Have you ever heard of Charles Finney, the preacher from the middle 1800s? He was converted to Christ by reading Blackstone's law commentaries. Blackstone had a clear Christian worldview. He was a proponent of natural law which is based on Romans 1, which says that there are two ways of God revealing himself. God reveals Himself through the Bible and through nature. While checking out the Founders, check out Blackstone. Finney did and became a Christian because of it. Wythe believed that God revealed Himself in the Bible and through nature. At the end of his life, Wythe studied Hebrew so that he could understand more of God's revelation in the Old Testament better.

Wythe was known for his integrity. He would not take a case where he knew the defendant was guilty. In Imogene Brown's biography, American Aristedes, there is a telling illustration. Wythe's seal was a judge who accepted a bribe, for which Cambyses had him killed and flayed, and his skin was cut into strips and stretched across the judicial seat. Sisamnes's son Otanes, was then appointed judge and told to remember the seat on which he sat to administer justice. It was a daily reminder that he sat, incorruptible, upon the seat of Sisamnes.

Wythe was on a committee (along with Thomas Stone and Robert Treat Paine) that prepared the oath of officers of the army and navy.

"...So help me God..."
"Resolved, That every officer who holds, or shall hereafter hold, shall subscribe the above declaration and take the foregoing oath."

"Resolved, that it is the opinion of this committee that Mr. Samuel Kirkland and Mr. Aaron Crosby, whom the commissioners at

Boston, appointed by the society for propagating the gospel among the Indians, had employed as missioners for that purpose, the former at Oneida, the other at Onaguache, be continued in their offices one year from the expiration of that for which they are now engaged; and that each of them be allowed a salary of four hundred and sixteen dollars and two thirds of a dollar...George Wythe writing on behalf of committee on Indian affairs (Journals of Cont. Congress, VI, 984).

Richard Henry Lee

Richard Henry Lee was born a month earlier than George Washington and just a few miles away. He was sent at an early age to study in England. He formed a corps under General Braddock in 1755. Braddock exemplified the British attitude toward the colonists and did not allow Lee's group to fight, nor did he heed Washington's advice about Indian strategy. "What, an American bushkin teach a British general how to fight?" Richard was the first Virginian to oppose the Stamp Act. He also suggested Committees of Correspondence in 1768. On June 7, 1776 he introduced the resolution for a separation from the mother country. Like Patrick Henry, it took courage to mention the unmentionable.

Richard Henry Lee's Draft Address to the People of Great Britain, June 27, 1775

> "Great cause therefore hath all men to bless God, who put it into the heads and hearts of our Countrymen to possess themselves of the fortresses of Ticonderoga and Crown Point, and to make themselves masters of those lakes that cover the frontiers of many Colonies… We call to witness, that it is the earnest wish of our hearts to be firmly united with you on the broad basis of civil and religious liberty equally, extended to all the subjects of this great empire."

Richard Henry Lee to Catherine Macaulay, Nov. 29, 1775

> "…As a good Christian properly attached to your native Country, I am sure you must be pleased to hear that North America is not fallen, nor likely to fall down before the Image that the King has set up."

Richard Henry Lee to Arthur Lee (Feb.11, 1779) XII, 56.

> "…God of his infinite mercy grant it may be so."

Richard Henry Lee to Unknown (October 22, 1776), V, 365

"...May Heaven prosper your righteous consultations and give success to the virtuous cause of America."

Richard Henry Lee to William Lee (September 20, 1775) I, p. 88.

"It seems to me, that if Ministry have not their hearts hardened, as the Scripture has it, they will best consult the good of their Country and their own safety by a prudent and speedy reversal."

Thomas Jefferson

Thomas Jefferson's father died when Thomas was fourteen years old. Being the oldest of eight children, Thomas inherited the estate. A Scottish clergyman named Douglas taught him from age 9 to 14. After his father's death, the Reverend Maury became his teacher. In 1760 he studied at William and Mary under George Wythe. He was a member of the Continental Congress starting in 1775. He wrote the Declaration of Independence. In June 1779 he succeeded Patrick Henry as governor of Virginia. While he was governor, the British almost captured Jefferson. From 1784 to 1789 he was in Paris, France. Please note that he was absent during the Constitutional Convention. In 1796 he was elected Vice-President and in 1800, President. He and John Adams both died on the 50th anniversary of the Fourth of July in 1826.

<u>Thomas Jefferson, Query XVIII, 1781 [engraved on Jefferson Memorial]</u>

> "God who gave us life gave us liberty. And can the liberties of a nation be though secure when we have removed their only firm basis, a conviction in the minds of the people that these liberties are of the gift of God? That they are not to be violated but with his wrath? Indeed, I tremble for my country when I reflect that God is just; that His justice cannot sleep forever."

<u>Thomas Jefferson to Edmund Pendleton (August 26, 1776) V, 66.</u>

> "... The fantastical idea of virtue and the public good being a sufficient security to the state against the commission of crimes, which you say you have heard insisted on by some, I assure you was never mine. It is only the sanguinary hue of our penal laws which I meant to object to Punishments I know are necessary and I would provide them, strict and inflexible, but proportioned to the crime. Death might be inflicted for murder and perhaps for treason all crimes which

are not such in their nature. rape, buggery &c. punish by castration."

Thomas Jefferson, A Bill for Establishing Religious Freedom, 1777

"...Almighty God hath created the mind free...No man shall be compelled to frequent or support any religious worship or ministry or shall otherwise suffer on account of his religious opinions or belief, but all men shall be free to profess and by argument to maintain, their opinions in matters of religion."

Benjamin Harrison

Benjamin Harrison was a student at William and Mary when his father died. Being the oldest of six sons, the management of the estate fell on him. In 1764 he became a member of the House of Burgesses and was later elected as Speaker. He was elected as a Virginia representative to the Continental Congress from 1774 to 1779. He became Speaker twice and governor. He married a niece of Mrs. Washington- Elizabeth Bassett. They had many children- one of whom became president- William Henry Harrison. He was also a cousin of Thomas Nelson, Jr. of Yorktown.

While signing the Declaration of Independence, Harrison noticed Eldridge Gerry of Massachusetts standing beside him. Mr. Harrison himself was quite big; Mr. Gerry was on the skinny side. As the former raised his hand, having inscribed his name on the roll, he turned to Mr. Gerry, and facetiously observed, that when the time of hanging should come, he should have the advantage over him. "It will be over with me," said he, "in a minute, but you will be kicking in the air half an hour after I am gone."

Benjamin Harrison to Robert Carter Nicolas, Feb. 13, 1776

"...I left New York on Wednesday last. (3) Genl. Clinton was then there and I believe on his way to Virga. to meet a fleet which he expected from England. He gave out that he was to go to the Southward but you must prepare for him, for I think he will most assuredly Stop with you, as he certainly intends to Hampton Road to wait for his Troops which are to rendeavous there. Should he land them God knows what will become of you even if you have your 9 Battalions Raised, for I understand you have not Arms for a Quarter part of them."

In 1769 Benjamin Harrison served on a "Committee of Religion" with Lewis Burwell, Thomas Nelson, Jr. and George Washington (Patriot Above Profit, p. 136.

Thomas Nelson, Jr.

Thomas Nelson, Jr. was sent to England at age 14 to get an education. He finished his studies at Cambridge (Trinity College) in 1761 under Dr. Proteus, who later became Bishop of London. Thomas was elected a member of the House of Burgesses of Virginia. He proposed the almost treasonable measure of organizing the militia of Virginia for the defense of the chartered rights of the people. He served at the Continental Congress until 1777 when health caused him to resign. He raised a volunteer corps in Virginia at his own expense. Nelson became governor of Virginia in 1781. In the movie "Patriot," there is a 5 second part which shows the bombing of Nelson's home (which was used by Cornwallis and his staff). During the siege of Yorktown, Nelson gave permission to have his house bombarded. One can see cannonballs in the bricks in his reconstructed house.

Thomas Nelson, Jr. to Mann Page; Jan. 4, 1776

> "…Our obtaining Victories with so little, or I may say without any loss at all, is certainly a proof of our being under the immediate protection of Providence."

Thomas Nelson, Jr. to John Page; Feb. 13, 1776

> "What think you of the Right Revd. Fathers in God the Bishops? One of them refused to ordain a young Gentleman, who went from America, because he was a rebellious American, so that unless we will submit to Parliamentary oppression, we shall not have the gospel preached among us. As a member of the Church of England I am sorry for it, but let every Man worship God under his own Fig Tree."

Thomas Nelson, Jr. served on a "Committee of Religion" for the state of Virginia in 1769 and 1771 (Patriot Above Profit, p. 136)

Thomas Nelson, Jr., Floor of House of Delegates, March 23, 1775

"I am a merchant of York Town, but I am a Virginian first. Let my trade perish. I call God to witness that if any British troops are landed in the County of York, of which I am lieutenant, I will wait for no orders, but will summon the militia and drive the invaders into the sea."

Francis Lightfoot Lee

Francis Lightfoot Lee was the younger brother of Richard Henry Lee. Francis was not able to go to England for education because of his father's death. He was educated nearby under the care of Rev. Doctor Craig, a Scottish clergyman. In 1765, Francis was elected to the House of Burgesses, representing Loudon County where he stayed until 1772. He then married the daughter of Colonel John Taylor of Richmond and moved there. He became a delegate to the Continental Congress. He represented Virginia there until 1777.

Francis Lightfoot Lee to John Page; Jan. 30, 1776

"There are English Papers in this City brought by a Ship from Dunkirk, which mention Mr. Penn, who carried the last Petition to the King, being examined before the House of Lords. His answers were short and clever, and seemed to have weight with some of that Body, who had before been in the Dark. The expression is that he had made several of them Quakers. The Duke of Grafton, the Archbishops of Canterbury, and the bishop of Peterborough have espoused the American cause." [This shows how religious leaders in England were coming to our side]

Francis Lightfoot Lee to Landon Carter; Jan. 14, 1777

"...Don't you give us credit for our good policy in removing from Philadelphia? Nothing else could awaken the Whigs of that State to a sense of their danger. The lethargy of the middle States was really alarming; thank God! It is removed, our new Army once well on foot & all is safe, but I believe, my friend, we must be content with homespun the rest of our lives."

Francis Lightfoot Lee to Landon Carter (November 20, 1775), II, 365-366.

"...The transports from Ireland with five Regiments compleat have arrived from Boston, a fishing boat with a schooner belonging to the fleet loaded with provisions for the officers, in her were many letters by which we learn that the Roman Catholic Lords, Bishops and Gentry are extreamly active in procuring recruits; the Protestants very averse to the business, man recruiting parties driven out of their towns, and even the lower class of Catholics show great dislike to it, but with the high premiums given by the Popish towns &c. many recruits are raised... The establishment of Popery will no doubt, be the reward of the exertions of the Roman catholics."

Carter Braxton

Carter Braxton's parents died when he was young. He was educated at William and Mary. After graduating, he married Judith Robinson. Judith died at the birth of their second child at age 20. Carter took a trip to England in 1757 and when he returned in 1760, he married the daughter of Mr. Corbin who was the royal receiver-general of the customs of Virginia. He had strong ties to British power but still kept the beat of patriotism. In December 1775 he was elected to fill the seat of Peyton Randolph (who had served as President of Continental Congress). He served in the Virginia Assembly from 1769 to 1785 except for the 1776 session.

Carter Braxton to Landon Carter; May 17, 1776

"...What then will be the consequence God only knows."

Carter Braxton to Landon Carter [uncle], April 14, 1776

"Two of the new England Colonies enjoy a Government purely democratical the Nature & Principle of which both civil & religious are so totally incompatible with Monarchy that they have ever lived in a restless State under it. The other two tho not so popular in their frame bordered so near upon it that Monarchical Influence hung very heavy on them. The best opportunity in the World being now offered them to throw off all Subjection & embrace their darling Democracy, they are determined to accept it."

Samuel Chase

Samuel Chase was born near Princess Anne, Maryland. His father was an Anglican minister who moved to Baltimore when Samuel was two years old. His father taught him at home. At age eighteen, Samuel was sent to Annapolis to study law and after two years he was admitted to practice in the mayor's court. In 1761 he was chosen as a member of the Provincial Assembly where he lifted his voice against the Stamp Act. He was chosen as a delegate to Continental Congress and stayed until 1778. In 1788 he was appointed Chief Justice of the Supreme Court of Maryland. In 1796 he was appointed as a U.S. Supreme Court justice. He was impeached but was acquitted.

<u>Samuel Chase to James Duane; Feb. 5, 1775</u>

> "...The Roman Senate in the Reign of Claudius Caesar, Domitian or Nero were not more severely wicked than the present House of Commons. They no longer regard even the Appearance of Virtue. Our Dependence must be on God & ourselves."

<u>Samuel Chase to Philip Schuyler; Aug. 9, 1776</u>

> "...I hope Heaven has heard my prayers, & your friendly wishes. I expect to find one of the best of women & of wifes in a much better State of Health, than when I was compelled to leave her...Our day of Trial approaches, God grant us Success, or our Country is undone."

<u>Samuel Chase, Chief Justice of the State of Maryland;
1799 Runkel v. Winemiller</u>

> "By our form of government, the Christian religion is the established religion; and all sects and denominations of Christians are placed upon the same footing, and are equally entitled to protection in their religious liberty."

Samuel Chase to John Dickinson (Feb. 6, 1775) I,

"Our dependence must be on God and Ourselves."

Samuel Chase to Philip Schuyler; (August 10, 1775), I, 700.

"God grant you success."

William Paca

William Paca was born at Wye Hall on the Eastern Shore of Maryland. He studied at Philadelphia College. Like Chase, he was chosen as a member of the Provincial Assembly in 1761. Paca, Chase and Carroll strongly opposed the Stamp Act. Paca was elected to the Continental Congress from 1774 to 1778 when he was appointed Chief Justice of the State of Maryland. In 1782 he became governor of the state. He was judge for the federal district of Maryland from 1789 until his death in 1799.

An unnamed acquaintance provided a description of his last hours: (from Stiverson, Gregory A. and Phoebe R. Jacobsen. William Paca: A Biography),

> "During his illness he conversed with perfect resignation on his approaching dissolution and cheerfully submitted to sickness and death under a deep conviction of the unerring wisdom and goodness of his heavenly Father and of the redemption of the world by our Lord and Saviour Jesus Christ. To the faith and charity of a Christian he added the civil virtues of a gentleman."

As Chief Justice of the State of Maryland in 1782:
Official recommendation to the General Assembly:

"It is far from our intention to embarrass your deliberations with a variety of objects, but we cannot pass over matters of so high concernment as religion and learning. The sufferings of the ministers of the gospel of all denominations, during the war, have been very considerable, and the perseverance and firmness of those who discharged their sacred functions under many discouraging circumstances, claim our acknowledgments and thanks. The bill of rights and form of government recognize the principle of public support for the ministers of the gospel, and ascertain the mode. Anxiously solicitous for the blessings of government, and the welfare and happiness of our citizens, and thoroughly convinced of the powerful influence of religion, when diffused by its respectable teachers, we beg leave most seriously and warmly to recommend among the first objects of your attention on the return of peace, the making such provision as the constitution, in this case, authorizes and approves."

GOD SAVE THE STATE

Thomas Stone

The details of Thomas Stone's life can sometimes be sketchy. His father was a descendant of William Stone, who was governor of Maryland during the protectorate of Oliver Cromwell. Thomas was born in Pointoin Hall in Charles County, Maryland and at age 21 started practicing law in Annapolis. In 1774 he was one of the Maryland delegates to the Continental Congress. Maryland had a hard time choosing for or against independence. The Maryland delegation instructed their delegates <u>not</u> to vote for independence. The restriction was lifted in June 1776 and Maryland voted for independence. He was president of Congress, pro tempore.

In 1787, Mrs. Stone died, after having a smallpox inoculation. Doctors recommended that Mr. Stone take a voyage. He died of a heart attack at the dock in Alexandria, Virginia.

<u>Thomas Stone to James Hollyday; May 20, 1776</u>

> "...The illness of a wife I esteem so dearly preys most severely on my Spirits, she is I thank God something better this afternoon, and this Intermission of her Disorder affords me Time to write to you. The Doctr. Thinks she is in a fair way of being well in a few days. I wish I thought so... May God attend our Deliberations & Direct them to the right way."

<u>Thomas Stone to the Maryland Council of Safety; July 12, 1776</u>

> "...May God send Victory to the Arm lifted in Support of righteousness, Virtue & Freedom and crush even to destruction the power which would eventually trample on the rights of mankind."

Thomas Stone worked on a committee along with George Wythe and Robert Treat Paine that prepared the oaths of officers of the army and navy.

"...So help me God."

"Resolved, That every officer who holds, or shall subscribe the above declaration and take the foregoing oath."
Journals of Continental Congress, VI, 887; Oct. 21, 1776

Charles Carroll

Charles Carroll is the only Roman Catholic signer of the Declaration of Independence. His education was in France and the Temple in London. Being one of the richest merchants in the American colonies, Carroll argued sharply against the Stamp Act. In 1772 he wrote a series of essays against the British taxation of the colonies under the name "The First Citizen." He was known as being in favor of independence early on and this hurt his chances of being elected in Maryland's environment. Carroll was on a committee with Franklin and others sent to Canada to get them to join us. He spent many years as a Maryland state Senator. He was the last signer to die, in 1832.

<u>Charles Carroll of Carrollton to Charles Carroll, Sr.; Aug.1, 1776</u>

"…We are making preparations to burn the enemy's ships at New York: God send our attempt may succeed."

<u>Charles Carroll of Carrollton to James McHenry; Nov. 4, 1800</u>

"…Without morals a republic cannot subsist any length of time; they therefore who are decrying the Christian religion, whose morality is so sublime and pure,…are undermining the solid foundation of morals, the best security for the duration of a free government."

<u>Charles Carroll of Carrollton to Charles Carroll, Sr.; May 30, 1777</u>

"My love to Molly, Mrs. Darnall & the little ones. God grant you health & a long enjoyment of it. I am, Yr. affectionate Son, Ch. **Carroll** of Carrollton"

"Too much of my time & attention have been misapplied on matters to which an impartial Judge, penetrating the secret of hearts, before whom I shall soon appear, will ascribe merit deserving recompense. *On the mercy of my redeemer I rely for salvation and on his merits; not on the works I have done in obedience to his precepts* [emphasis mine], for even these, I fear, a fallacy a mixture will render unavailing, and cause to be rejected." Charles Carroll, September 27, 1825

Caesar Rodney

Caesar Rodney was born in 1730. His mother was the daughter of a minister. Caesar started in the legislature in 1762. He was a delegate to the Stamp Act Congress, and showed his opposition to the bill. By 1769 he was chosen Speaker of the Provincial Assembly, where he stayed until 1774. He, along with McKean and Read, was chosen to be a representative at the Continental Congress. Rodney was there for much of the debate for independence but was sick when the vote was coming up. McKean was for independence but Read was against. McKean sent a courier to get Rodney in order to break the tie. Rodney, still sick, rode through the night in a storm from Dover to Philadelphia and arrived just in time to cast a deciding vote for independence. General Rodney led the Delaware army for a while. Cancer in the cheek was the cause of his death in 1783.

Caesar Rodney to Thomas Rodney; Sept. 11, 1776

> "...The Israelites (the Chosen People of God) met with crosses and disappointments in their Journey from the land [of] Bondage to that of Liberty, But by a Steady perseverance and divine assistance they at length possessed the promised Land. So that, that God Who Vieweth & Judgeth all things with Unerring Wisdom, Seeing the Righteousness of his Cause (tho he permitted Temporary Obstruction) Will one day (with a firm Reliance on him) Crown his Virtuous Endeavours with Success, and Cause the Modern Pharaoh's with their hosts to be buried in the Sea of their Toryism, as he did the Antient Pharaoh in the Red Sea."

Caesar Rodney to Thomas Rodney (July 10, 1776) IV, 433

> "... But Sir, now is the time and Season that our open and avowed Enemies are pressing hard. They call forth the attention and Utmost Vigilence of the Congress to that Point. They well know they have internal Enemies in disguise, and Whenever, by the blessing of God, their Virtuous Efforts

Shall be Crowned with Success, They will immediately turn thoughts towards those Sappers of the Rights of Mankind."

Caesar Rodney to Thomas Rodney (Dec. 7, 1775) II, 451

"...I am extremely Sorry that Betsey has been and continued to bee so ill when you last wrote. God grant Shee may get better."

George Read

George Read was from Irish background and grew up in Newcastle County. He studied under Rev. Dr. Allison at the College of Philadelphia. He was admitted to the bar to practice law in 1753. That same year his father died. As the eldest son he was entitled to two shares of his father's estate, but he relinquished all his rights in favor of his brothers. His reason for this was that his education was his portion. In 1763 he was appointed attorney general of the three counties on the Delaware. He was elected to serve at the Continental Congress in 1774. Mr. Read voted against the declaration but supported it when the measure passed and even took a part in the militia.

George Read to Gertrude Read; July 14, 1776

"…Banish your fears, all may be right. A few weeks will discover much, I hope in our favor. God preserve you and believe me yours affectionately."

Delaware Convention, August 31, 1776 (George Read, President)

"1. That each Member of this Convention take the following Oath or Affirmation, that is to say;
I, A. B. [able-bodied] will to the utmost of my Power support and maintain the Independence of this State as declared by the Honorable the Continental Congress; and I will to the utmost of my Ability endeavor to form such a System of Government for the People of this State as in my Opinion may be best adapted to promote their Happiness and secure to them the Enjoyment of their natural, civil and religious Rights and Privileges.
2. That every Member make and subscribe the following Declaration, to wit.
'I, A. B. do profess Faith in God the Father, and in Jesus Christ his only Son, and in the Holy Ghost, one God blessed for evermore.'"

Thomas McKean to George Read (April 3, 1778), IX, 363.

"… I congratulate you on the whig election in Sussex."

Thomas McKean

Thomas McKean was born in New London in Chester County in Pennsylvania in 1734. After studying with Rev. Allison at the University of Philadelphia, he became a lawyer. McKean later became Chief Justice of Pennsylvania and also the President of Delaware. In 1781, he was President of the Continental Congress. He kept his job as Chief Justice of Pennsylvania for 22 years until 1799.

In 1777, McKean had to move his family five times to avoid British troops. McKean was instrumental in the original constitutions of Delaware and Pennsylvania.

<u>Thomas McKean to Nathanael Greene, July 26, 1781</u>

"…When the most virtuous Cause that ever a People was engaged in is conducted by consummate Providence and Wisdom, supported by Fortitude and true Courage, and visibly favored by the Almighty, there are the surest Grounds to expect Success.

"That you may give Peace, Liberty and Independence to the Southern State, whose sufferings, Bravery, and determined Conduct prove them to be entirely deserving of these Blessings, is the most ardent Prayer of, Sir, Your most obedient and most humble servant."

<u>Thomas McKean, Chief Justice of Pennsylvania, Republica vs. John Roberts</u>

"You will probably have but a short time to live. Before you launch into eternity, it behooves you to improve the time that may be allowed you in this world. It behooves you most seriously to reflect upon your conduct, to repent of your evil deeds, to be incessant in prayers to the great and merciful God to forgive your manifold transgressions and sins, to teach you to rely upon the merit and passion of a dear Redeemer and thereby to avoid those regions of sorrow, those doleful shades where peace and rest can never dwell, where even hope cannot enter. It behooves you to seek the fellowship, advice and prayers of pious and good men, to be persistent at the throne of grace and to learn the way that leadeth to happiness. May you reflecting upon these things and pursuing the will of the great Father of Light and Life, be received into the company and society of angels and archangels and the spirits of just men made perfect and may you be qualified to enter into the joys of heaven, joys unspeakable and full of glory."

Robert Morris

Robert Morris was one of the richest men in America at the time of the American Revolution. He and Thomas Willing owned the largest importing house in Philadelphia. When the Stamp Act and Tea act passed, Morris and Willing "willingly" went with non-importation agreements. When Morris heard of the tragedy of Lexington, he made a vow with others to dedicate his life, fortune and honor to the cause of liberty for America. In 1781 Congress was in financial straits. Congress could not obtain a loan of $100,000, yet Robert Morris worked out loans upon his own credit of tens of thousands of dollars. Because of later financial speculation, Robert Morris died a pauper.

Robert Morris to William Bingham; Feb. 26, 1777

> "...You will have seen by former advices that Kind Providence gave a change to the affairs of America on Christmas Night when Gen. Washington begun an attempt to surprise Trenton which he effected the next morning & took Prisoners three Hessian Regiments."

Robert Morris to George Washington; Feb. 27, 1777

> "...Heaven (no doubt for the noblest purposes) has blessed you with a Firmness of mind, Steadiness of Countenance and patience in sufferings that give you infinite Advantages over other men."

Robert Morris to John Jay; Feb. 4, 1777

> "...God bless you and grant success to America in the present Contest."

Robert Morris to John Jay (Jan. 12, 1777), VI, 87-88

> "...Where it will end God only knows... What a glorious change in our prospects. Pray heaven Continue our Success and grant me an opportunity of Congratulation you on regaining the City of New York."

Secret Committee to Robert Morris (Dec. 23, 1776), V, 651

> "... God grant the enemy may fail in their scheme against your City."

Robert Morris to John Hancock (Feb. 21, 1777) VI, 339

> "...I have really had my hands, Head & Heart full of business since I saw you but thank God my Spirits never failed."

Benjamin Rush

Many biographies of Benjamin Rush will document his many accomplishments in medicine, philosophy, philanthropy, etc. but will neglect the Christian faith of the man. His writings on Biblical reasons why one should be a doctor are highly recommended for today's readers. He started the Philadelphia Bible Society and was a mover and a shaker in the American Bible Society.

Benjamin Rush to Julia Rush; Sept. 18-25, 1776

> "...My faith is now stronger than ever. I begin to hear with pleasure an outcry among some people that there is to be no dependence to be had upon the arm of the flesh. But the worst is not over. We must be bro't lower. I predict a defeat or another disgraceful retreat. We stand in need of it. We must all be taught that 'Salvation is not to be hoped from the hills, nor from the multitude of the Mountains,' before we can prevail over our enemies."

Benjamin Rush to Julia Rush; Jan. 31, 1777

"...There are a number of boarders in the family. One of them is a young French officer. His story is one particular is very remarkable. He is one of one and twenty children, 18 boys and 3 girls. They were all born of the same father & mother, and are all now living. Happy family! I shall be better satisfied if the same can be said [of] me as was said of the prophet of old 'That I walked in the ways of the Lord, and begat sons and daughters,' than if it were inscribed upon my tombstone that I governed the counsels, or commanded the arms of the whole continent of America."

Constitution of Philadelphia Bible Society, which Rush wrote

"...the inestimable value of the revelation which it hath pleased God to make to our world of His existence, character, will, works and grace in Jesus Christ in the Bible, and of the great benefits to be expected from the distribution of it among persons who are unable or not disposed to purchase it,... a Society for that purpose, to be called The Bible Society."

"...My only hope of salvation is in the infinite, transcendent love of God manifested to the world by the death of His Son upon the Cross. Nothing but His blood will wash away my sins. I rely exclusively upon it. Benjamin Rush, The Autobiography of Benjamin Rush, George Corner, editor (Princeton: Princeton University Press, 1948), p. 166.

Benjamin Franklin

The focus of many character sketches about Ben Franklin highlight some of his negative points and neglect the overall good effect of his life. Many of these character sketches tell us about worldview of the writer that the writer wishes to push instead of Mr. Franklin. In our present society, here is what revisionist writers want you to know: Franklin was a ladies' man and was a deist, end of story. He was a worldly wise scientist and politician. Let's spend some time with Mr. Franklin.

<u>Benjamin Franklin to David Hartley; Oct. 3, 1775</u>

"I am persuaded that the body of the British people are our friends; but they are changeable, and by your lying gazettes may soon be made our enemies. Our respect for them will proportionately diminish, and I see clearly we are on the high road to mutual family hatred and detestation. A separation of course will be inevitable. It is a million of pities so fair a plan as we have hitherto been engaged in, for increasing strength and empire with public felicity, should be destroyed by the mangling hands of a few blundering ministers. It will not be destroyed; God will protect and prosper it, you will only exclude yourselves from any share in it. We hear, that more ships and troops are coming out. We know, that you may do us a great deal of mischief, and are determined to bear it patiently as long as we can. But if you flatter yourselves with beating us into submission, you know neither the people nor the country."

<u>Benjamin Franklin at the Constitutional Convention, June 28, 1787</u>

"I have lived, Sir, a long time, and the longer I live, the more convincing proofs I see of this truth: that God governs in the affairs of man. And if a sparrow cannot fall to the ground without his notice, is it probable that an empire can rise without His aid? We have been assured, Sir, in the Sacred

Writings that 'except the Lord build the house, they labor in vain that build it.' I firmly believe this..."

Benjamin Franklin's Vindication (June- July, 1775) I, 563

"Our own arms, with our poverty, and the care of a kind Providence, were all this time our only protection."

John Morton

John Morton was born in 1724 in Ridley, Pennsylvania. From Swedish ancestry, John grew up on a farm. John's father died when John was young. His stepfather, John Sketchley, an Englishman, saw to his education and helped him get into surveying. Not only was he from Swedish background, John went on to marry a young woman from Swedish background as well- Ann Justice. They had three sons and five daughters.

He was elected to the provincial assembly in 1756 and eventually became Speaker of the House. He was a delegate at the 1st and 2nd Continental Congress (1774 and 1775). He initially voted against independence but saw that the offers of reconciliation were useless. He cast the deciding vote for Pennsylvania. He joined Franklin and Wilson voting for independence as Willing and Humphrey voted against it. Morton died in less than a year- in April 1777.

John Morton

(John Morton's Will)
>"With an awful reference to the Great Almighty God, Creator of all mankind, being sick and weak in body but sound in mind and memory, thanks be given to Almighty God for the same."

John Morton to Persifor Frazer, August, 18, 1776

>"...I had almost forgot to mention the arrival of Devil Dunmore and Clinton who are both at N York and all their troops. With my best Respects to you and prayers for your health."

George Clymer

George Clymer was orphaned at an early age and was reared by his uncle. The uncle apprenticed him as a merchant.

He was one of the first members of Pennsylvania's committee of safety and one of the first to advocate independence from Britain. He served as the first treasurer for the Continental Congress. He was not known as a good speaker but was known for his work in committees, especially assisting General Washington's army.

In 1782 Mr. Clymer moved his family to Princeton so his children could get their education there. Keep in mind that Princeton at that time had as its motto: "Under God's Power She Flourishes!" At present, no quotes can be found about his Christian worldview but he is implicated because of the Pennsylvania Constitution stipulation and the desire to teach his children to be Christians.

Pennsylvania Constitution (September 28, 1776) Section 10.

"...And each member, before he takes his seat, shall make and subscribe the following declaration, viz:

I do believe in one God, the creator and governor of the universe, the rewarder of the good and the punisher of the wicked. And I do acknowledge the Scriptures of the Old and New Testament to be given by Divine inspiration."

And no further or other religious test shall hereafter be required of any civil officer or magistrat in this State."

Mr. Clymer put his money where his mouth was. He exchanged his gold for Continental Currency. Patriot Before Profit, p. 325.

"I, A. B. do solemnly swear that I will truly and faithfully execute the office of commissioner to which I am appointed, according to my best skill and judgment, without favor or affection. So help me God."

Report of committee on commissioners before each is appointed, in the writing of George Clymer, Journals of Continental Congress, XXII, 86; Papers of Continental Congress, No. 26, folio 327.

James Smith

James Smith was born in Dublin, Ireland around 1719. His family moved to Cheshire County in Pennsylvania when he was about 10-12 years old. He was educated by Rev. Dr. Allison of the College of Philadelphia. Similar to George Ross, James studied law at his brother's law firm (which was also in Lancaster, Pennsylvania). At age 26 he set up a law office near Shippensburg. Smith was a captain in the Pennsylvania militia and in 1782 became Brigadier General of the militia.

In 1774 he wrote "Essay on the Constitutional Power of Great Britain Over the Colonies in America." In this essay he discussed a boycott of British goods and a General Congress of the Colonies. He became a member of the Continental Congress after the Declaration of Independence was signed. In his home area of York, Pennsylvania, Smith was colonel of a regiment. In 1782 he was appointed Brigadier General of the Pennsylvania militia. A fire in his office destroyed his papers shortly before his death in 1806. He was buried in the First Presbyterian Churchyard in York, Pennsylvania.

"On September 8, 1789, James Smith was one of three elders who attended the meeting of the Presbytery of Carlisle held at the Lower Marsh Creek Church. On August 6, 1792 a call was extended by the congregation to Reverend Robert Cathcart, who was born in Ireland and educated at the University of Glasgow, and who had come to America several years before. James Smith was one of the signers of this call." William B. Miller, "Presbyterian Signers of the Declaration of Independence", Journal of the Presbyterian Historical Society, p. 146.

George Taylor

George Taylor was another son of a minister in Ireland. It appears that George came to Pennsylvania as an indentured servant or close to it. He had to pay for his passage and worked for a Mr. Savage. This Mr. Savage was the owner of an iron works at Durham on the Delaware River, near Easton. When Mr. Savage died years later, George married his widow. The business went well and George became a member of the provincial assembly from 1764 until 1770 when the business was having difficulties. He returned to the assembly in 1775. Pennsylvania was torn between independence and staying tied with England. In 1775, the assembly members were admonished to do their utmost to preserve peace while addressing the grievances. The winds changed in 1776. Here is how the assembly charged the delegates (and Taylor was one):

"The happiness of these colonies has, during the whole course of this fatal controversy, been our first wish. Their reconciliation with Great Britain our next. Ardently have we prayed for the accomplishment of both. But if we must renounce the one or the other, we humbly trust in the mercies of the Supreme Governor of the universe, that we shall not stand condemned before his throne, if our choice is determined by that overruling law of self-preservation, which His divine wisdom has thought fit to implant in the hearts of his creatures."

He was not present at the signing of the Declaration of Independence. He arrived July 20, 1776 but would have voted for it had he been there.

"On March 8, 1765 a lot of approximately one acre of land in Springfield Township was given for the Presbyterian minister to Richard Treat and George Taylor & to their heirs and assigns for Ever in trust for a burying ground...for sole use benefit & Behoof, of the Presbyterian Congregation in Tineeum Township." William B. Miller, "Presbyterian

Signers of the Declaration of Independence," Journal of the Presbyterian Historical Society, XXXVI; 1958, No. 3, p. 147.

James Wilson

James Wilson was born and educated in Scotland. He arrived in Philadelphia in 1766 and was helped by Bishop William White and Judge Peters to enter the law office of John Dickinson. Amongst the Pennsylvania delegates Wilson, Franklin and Morton voted for independence while Humphreys and Willing voted against while Dickinson and Morris were absent.

(Delegates Certification of James Wilson's Conduct in Congress, June 20, 1776)

> "We, the Subscribers, Members of Congress do therefore certify, that in a late Debate in this House upon a Proposition to declare these Colonies free and independent States, Mr. Wilson after having selected the Progress of the Dispute between Great Britain and the Colonies, declared it to be his opinion that the Colonies would stand justified before God and the World in declaring an absolute Separation from Great Britain forever."

(The Works of James Wilson, Vol. I, pp. 104-106, of the General Principles of Law and Obligation)

> "Human law must rest its authority ultimately upon the authority of that law which is divine...Far from being rivals or enemies, religion and law are twin sisters, friends, and mutual assistants. Indeed, these two sciences run into each other."
>
> "...Do what it is in your Power to do; and you have the greatest Reason to rest assured that, under the gracious Protection of divine Providence, your virtuous Struggles will be crowned with abundant Success." Report in the writing of James Wilson, Journals of Continental Congress, VIII, p. 404. (In the Papers of the Continental Congress, No. 24, folio 238).

Wilson was one of twelve appointed to form a corporation and govern the Society of Presbyterians of the First Presbyterian Church in the Centre Square near the court house in the town of Carlisle. He financially supported the First Presbyterian Church in Philadelphia (gave 100 pounds for its restoration after the war, rented a pew every year from 1778 until his death in 1798). William B. Miller, "Presbyterian Signers of the Declaration of Independence," Journal of the Presbyterian Historical Society, XXXVI; 1958, No. 3, p. 147.

George Ross

George Ross was one of at least ten signers who were sons of ministers. When the inhabitants of Lancaster County (Pennsylvania) sent £150, Ross returned it. He said it was the duty of every man, and especially of every representative of the people to contribute by every means within his power, to the welfare of his country, without expecting pecuniary rewards.

George was educated at home. He became a lawyer through his brother's practice and went on to establish his own law practice in Lancaster. He served as Crown Prosecutor in Carlisle from 1756 to 1768. He was elected to the Pennsylvania Provincial Assembly from 1768 to 1776 and was sent to the Continental Congress in 1774, 1776 and 1777. He resigned late in 1777 due to poor health and died in 1779. He was related by marriage to Betsy Ross.

Benjamin Rush was baptized by Enna Ross, an Episcopal minister who was the brother of George Ross.

George Ross to James Wilson, Nov. 17, 1775

> "...I can't help saying Heaven seems to Smile on & favour the great cause of Liberty. Our Successes have been equal to our most sanguine hopes And I think nothing but our own misconduct can prevent our Triumphing over the Enemies of America"

George Ross to James Wilson, Nov. 26, 1776

> "The distress of our Soldiers who I have met almost naked and hardly able to walk or rather wade through the mud has given infinite pain but I shudder to tell you that they fall dead on the road with their packs on their backs or are found accidentally perishing in hay lofts. There has indeed been too much Inattention to the sick. Pray God forgive the negligence wherever it may be."

Richard Stockton

Richard Stockton graduated in the first class from Princeton College in 1748. He was admitted to the bar of New Jersey in 1754. By 1763 he received the degree of sergeant-at-law, a high distinction in English court. In 1766 he made a 15 month travel in England and Scotland and was instrumental in persuading John Witherspoon's wife Elizabeth to come to Princeton. Richard's sister married Francis Hopkinson.

Richard was captured by the British and suffered greatly in a prison. He died a month after his prison release.

Richard Stockton to Abraham Clark; Oct. 28, 1776

"For God's sake, my dear sir, upon the receipt of this, collect all the shoes and stockings you can, and send them off for Albany in light wagons...Therefore, I trust with the blessings of the Almighty God, that we shall disappoint their wicked and sanguinary purposes."

Richard Stockton's Will

"...And as my children will have frequent occasion of perusing this instrument and may probably be particularly impressed with the last words of their father, I think proper here not only to subscribe to the entire belief of the great and leading doctrines of the Christian religion, such as the being of God, the universal defection and depravity of human nature, the divinity of the person and the completeness of the redemption purchased by the blessed Saviour, the necessity of the operations of the Divine Spirit; of Divine faith accompanied with a habitual virtuous life, and the universality of the Divine Providence; but also in the bowels of a father's affection, to exhort and charge them that the fear of God is the beginning of wisdom, that the way of life held up in the Christian system is calculated for the most complete happiness that can be enjoyed in this mortal state."

Richard Stockton to Benjamin Rush (Oct. 13, 1776), V, 342

"...I am, thank God, in good health."

John Witherspoon

Rev. John Witherspoon was a lineal descendant of John Knox, the Scottish reformer. Witherspoon had many offers to be a minister in Dublin or Rotterdam or Dundee as well as an offer to be heir of a considerable fortune, provided that he remained in Scotland. Witherspoon arrived in America in 1768 to become president of Princeton University. He represented New Jersey at the Continental Congress from 1776 to 1779 and then from 1781 to 1782. His oldest son James was killed in the battle of Germantown.

Listen to the following letter from John to his son David on Feb. 2, 1777. What would the British do to John if he were caught by the British, would they ask him to preach a sermon?:

> "...I have been making inquiry into the conduct of the enemy, which has been dreadful. At Trenton they killed Mr. Roxburgh, Presbyterian minister at the Forks of Delaware. Though he fell down on his knees and begged his life, yet they pierced him through and through with their bayonets, and mangled him in a most shocking manner. Some of the people at Princeton say thought they were killing me, and boasted that they had done it when they came back. But this is certain- the fact of his death and the manner of it is beyond all doubt."

John Witherspoon to David Witherspoon; Feb. 12, 1777

> "...My first concern is that you should fear God; ...I pray you to remember that the fear of the Lord is the beginning of wisdom; and that it is high time for you both, personally to renew your baptismal engagements, and solemnly give yourselves to God- I pray earnestly that he may renew you in the spirit of your minds."

John Witherspoon to David Witherspoon (July 27, 1776) IV,

"...As the Distance between us is go great I must not omit my dear Child to put you in Mind to walk with fear of God. Give your self much to the Exercise of Prayer & if you desire to improve & perservere in that Duty. You must be punctual as to the times of it. Irregular people do nothing to purpose either in that or any other Respect."

Francis Hopkinson

Francis Hopkinson graduated from the University of Philadelphia in 1757. He was admitted to the bar to practice law in 1761. He composed the first secular song as an American in 1759. This secular music songwriter also <u>put all 150 Psalms to music</u>. He played the organ for Christ Church in Philadelphia for many years. Along with that job, he taught many young people how to sing psalms.

<u>Francis Hopkinson</u>

"As late beneath the hallowed roof I trod,
Where saints in holy rapture seek their God;
Where heart stund sinners suing Heav'n for grace,
With tears repentant consecrate the place.
Oh! how my soul was struck by what I saw
And shrunk within me in religious awe."
"Description of a Church," III, pp.59-60.

"...So shall th' admir'd celestial art
Raise and transport my ravish'd heart;
Exalt my soul and give my mind
Ideas of sublimer kind.
So great the bliss it seems to prove
There must be music too above.
That from the trumpet's silver sound,
Of winged arch-angels plac'd around
Thy burning throne- Oh! king of heav'n!
Most perfect harmony is giv'n!
Whilst happy saints in concert join
To make the music quite divine,
And with immortal voices sing
HOSANNAHS to their heav'nly KING."

"Ode on Music," II, p.6

Francis Hopkinson's "Miscellaneous Essays and Occasional Writings," published at Philadelphia, 1792

John Hart

The name John Hart means little to most people. He was a signer from New Jersey. When I think of the sacrifice of the signers, my first thought goes to John Hart. Hart's farm was ravaged, his timber destroyed. His cattle were butchered and used by the British army. He never saw his wife and 13 children again. He had to hide in caves and out in the open. He died in 1779.

John Hart's Will

"...Thanks be given unto Almighty God therefore, and knowing that it is appointed for all men once to die and after that the judgement.. principally, I give and recommend my soul into the hands of Almighty God who gave it and my body to be buried in a decent and Christian like manner.. to receive the same again at the general resurrection by the mighty power of God."

John Hart's Address on Oct. 5, 1776 in the Papers of William Livingston

"...We will look for the permanency and stability of our new government to Him who bringeth princes to nothing and teacheth senators wisdom."

"On August 29, 1735, Hart was received as a member of the Hopewell Presbyterian Church, and evidence can be noted of his contributing to the church's support as late as thirty four years after this date. When he died on April 26, 1779, he was buried in a private burying ground of a family friend. However, his body was later removed and buried in the Hopewell Baptist Churchyard which had received from him in 1771 a deed for the plot on which the church and burial ground were situated." William B. Miller, "Presbyterian Signers of the Declaration of Independence," Journal of the Presbyterian Historical Society, XXXVI; 1958, No. 3, p. 147.

Abraham Clark

Abraham Clark also knew of sacrifice. His two sons were captured and were on a prison ship. Not only was Clark a signer but he also attended the Constitutional Convention in 1787 and served in Congress from 1787 until 1794.

Abraham Clark to Elias Dayton; July 14,1776

"...Our Declaration of Independence I dare say you have seen. A few weeks will probably determine our fate. Perfect freedom or Absolute slavery. To some of us freedom or a halter. Our fates are in the hands of an Almighty God, to whom I can with pleasure confide my own; he can save us or destroy us; his Councils are fixed and cannot be disappointed, and all his designs will be Accomplished."

Abraham Clark to James Caldwell; August 2, 1776

"...I not only fear for New Jersey, but the Army at N. York. If the British Army should Land above them they could neither retreat or get Supplies. We have only to rely upon the Almighty, but that reliance is scarcely to be seen. At my coming to Congress, I moved for a Chaplain to Attend Prayers every morning which was carried- and some of my Starch brethren will scarcely forgive me for naming Mr. Duche. This I did knowing without such a one many would not Attend. He hath composed a form of Prayer Unexceptionable to all parties."

Abraham Clark to Elias Dayton (March 7, 1777), VI, 414

"...Our Friend Mr. Caldwells Services I am particularly Attentive to, but the wheels drag heavy, a Presbyterian Clergyman is not with some a Popular Name, and tho' I have the assurances of Congress in his favour I can promise Nothing but my best endeavours."

William Floyd

William was born into a wealthy family. While in his teens, his father died and he was put in charge of the family farm. He was a Congregational church member.

As a signer of the Declaration of Independence, William Floyd was hunted by the British. When the British occupied Long Island in August 1776, Mr. Floyd's family had to flee on a ship to Connecticut. His wife Hannah died in May 1781 (possibly due in part to the stress and hardship of having to flee to Connecticut). Floyd married Joanna Strong in 1783. After the war he acquired land on the Mohawk River.

William Floyd to George Clinton, Feb. 20, 1779

"The money which I Rec'd as of our Treasurer for the Purpose of Bearing my Expenses here, happened to be mostly of the two Emitions which were put out of Circulation about the time I arrived here. Some of it I have Changed, the Rest I cannot, without a Loss of ten per Cent and God knows I am not in Circumstances to put it on Interest.

As a churchman Floyd was active in the incorporation of the South Haven Church in New York in 1802. At a meeting in January 19, 1802 in Samuel Carman's house, since there were no church-wardens elders Deacons or vestrymen belonging to said Parish or Congregation Wm. Floyd Esq. and Mr. Ebenezer Hart of said parish were named returning officers. William B. Miller, "Presbyterian Signers of the Declaration of Independence," Journal of the Presbyterian Historical Society, XXXVI; 1958, No. 3, p. 163.

"In testimony whereof, we have hereunto set our hands and seals, in the presence of Congress, the first of March, in the year of our Lord one thousand seven hundred and eighty-one and of our independence the fifth. James Duane, Wm. Floyd, Alexander McDougall"
Journal of Continental Congress, XX, p. 21, 213.

Philip Livingston

Philip Livingston was a great grandson of a minister of the Church of Scotland (Rev. John Livingstone). "Because of Reverend Livingstone's religion and opposition to the restoration of Charles II, he left Scotland and took charge of a Presbyterian congregation in Rotterdam. From such beginnings, Philip's roots in Presbyterianism had their roots." William B. Miller, "Presbyterian Signers of the Declaration of Independence," Journal of the Presbyterian Historical Society, XXXVI; 1958, No. 3, p. 101.

Edmund Burke's defense of the American cause in the British Parliament was largely due to the contact Burke had with Philip Livingston. Burke was the agent for New York and corresponded greatly with Livingston. Livingston died on June 12, 1778, while attending the Continental Congress at York, Pennsylvania.

Philip was the brother of William Livingston, the governor of New Jersey. William was the father-in-law of John Jay; Sally would call him Uncle Philip. Check out the story about "Give 'em Watts, Boys!" for some insights into William's faith. He graduated from Yale in 1737 and became a merchant in New York City. In 1754 Philip attended the Colonial Convention in Albany.

Philip worked on committees for commerce and navy affairs during the Revolution. He was instrumental in the founding of Kings College, the Society Library, Chamber of Commerce, served as one of the first governors of the New York Hospital, and president of the St. Andrew's Society.

According to Charles Goodrich (author of the Lives of the Signers to the Declaration of Independence, 1856), "He was a firm believer in the great truths of the Christian system, and a sincere and humble follower of the divine Redeemer." Philip also endowed a chair of theology at King's College. Most deists and atheists that I know would not fund a department of theology at a university where students had morning and evening prayers.

Francis Lewis

Francis Lewis not only was the son of a minister (Anglican) but his mother was the daughter of a minister. Francis was born in Llandaff, Wales in March 1713. At a young age, he became an orphan and was put under the care of his uncle, the dean of St. Paul's in London. He was educated at a Westminster school. He had a business in London, sold it in order to make investments which he brought with him to establish trade in New York and Philadelphia. Mr. Lewis lived through being a prisoner in the French and Indian War.

In the fall of 1776, Lewis' house was plundered. His wife fell prisoner to the British and died within two years. In 1779 he was appointed commissioner of the Board of Admiralty and was elected a vestryman of Trinity Church. Lewis spent the rest of his life in comparative poverty. His daughter married a British naval officer. His son Morgan became governor of New York in 1805, two years after Francis had died.

"And Whereas it hath pleased the Great Governor of the World to incline the hearts of the legislatures we respectively represent in congress, to approve of, and to authorize us to ratify the said articles of confederation and perpetual union…Done at Philadelphia in the state of Pennsylvania the ninth day of July, in the Year of our Lord one Thousand seven Hundred and Seventy-eight, and in the third year of the independence of America."

Francis Lewis, one of the signers of the Articles of Confederation, Journals of Continental Congress, XIX, p. 221-222.

Lewis Morris

Lewis Morris descended from a Richard Morris who was an officer of distinction under Cromwell. A Yale graduate, Morris entered early on the side of the patriot cause. He refused to take office under the Colonial government. New York was lukewarm on the issue of independence and the Tories did not want him at the Continental Congress in 1774. After Lexington and Concord, sentiments changed and he was elected in 1775. After signing the Declaration, three of Morris's sons entered the army. His house was ruined, his livestock was taken and his family had to flee. He lived amongst many wealthy Tory neighbors. He served as a Commissioner for Indian Affairs during the war. In 1777, his brother Gouveneur Morris succeeded him in Congress. Lewis spent many years trying to rebuild his farm.

Lewis Morris to Philip Schuyler; July 23, 1775

> "...I really feel for you under your present circumstances going upon a Dangerous expedition without Powder or good men. God send you success"

Lewis Morris to John Jay, March 8, 1777

> "The Congress meets to day for the first time since their flight. I wish to God we had more men in Jersey, you may be assured from the best authority Howe has not more than Seven Thousand Eight hundred Sick and well, shamefull to the Continent that they do not drive him out; however let us hope for the best."

Samuel Adams

Samuel Adams was in the vanguard of opposition to the Stamp Act and prepared the way for the Continental Congress to form. Political matters drove Samuel so much that his business matters suffered. He was the leader of a society called the Sons of Liberty, who were responsible for the Boston Tea Party. Listen to what the Father of the American Revolution had to say about the signing of the Declaration of Independence:

> "We have this day restored the Sovereign to Whom all men ought to be obedient. He reigns in heaven and from the rising to the setting of the sun, let His kingdom come."

<u>Samuel Adams to the Boston Committee of Correspondence; Sept. 16, 1774</u>

> "I hope the Committee will continue to Act up to their Dignity and Importance. I am yet of the opinion that Heaven will Honor them with a great share of the Merit of saving the Rights of America. May God inspire them with Wisdom & Fortitude... I conclude with the warmest prayers to the Supreme Being for the Salvation of our Country."

<u>Samuel Adams to James Warren, Dec. 12, 1776</u>

> "...I give up this City & State for lost until recoverd by other Americans. Our Cause however will be supported. It is the Cause of God & Men, and virtuous men by the Smiles of Heaven will bring it to a happy Issue...May God prosper them and increase their Number. Let America exert her own Strength. Let her depend upon God's Blessing, and He who cannot be indifferent to her righteous Cause will even work Miracles if necessary to carry her thro this glorious Conflict, and establish her feet upon a Rock. Adieu my Friend, the Clock strikes Twelve."

John Adams

Many of you have read David McCullough's excellent biography on John Adams. McCullough has done his homework. On page 19 he says:

"<u>Adams was both a devout Christian and an independent thinker and he saw no conflict in that.</u>"

McCullough included a letter Benjamin Rush sent to John Adams in his retirement years. Jefferson had opposed a proposal for a fast day and by doing so was putting down Christianity.

"You rose and defended the motion, and in reply to Mr. Jefferson's objections to Chrisitianity you said you were sorry to hear such sentiments from a gentleman whom you so highly respected and with whom you agreed on so many subjects, and that **it was the only instance you had ever known of a man of sound sense and real genious that was an enemy to Christianity.**"
(McCullough, p.113 quoted from Schutz and Adair, eds. Spur of Fame, p. 227.)
(emphasis mine)

<u>John Adams, June 28, 1813</u>

"Now I will avow, that I then believe, and now believe, that those general principles of Christianity, are as eternal and immutable [unchangeable], as the Existence and Attributes of God; and that those Principles of liberty, are as unalterable as human Nature and our terrestrial, mundane System."

<u>John Adams, June 21, 1776</u>

"Statesmen, my dear Sir, may plan and speculate for liberty, but it is Religion and Morality alone, which can establish the Principles upon which Freedom can securely stand."

Robert Treat Paine

Robert Treat Paine was another one of the signers whose father was a minister. Robert studied theology while at Harvard. He was a chaplain of troops during the French and Indian War. He was a delegate to the Massachusetts constitutional convention in 1779-1780 and was a judge on the Massachusetts supreme court from 1790 to 1804.

Here is a letter he wrote to Joseph Palmer on July 6, 1776 describing the Declaration of Independence:

"...Thus the issue is joined; and it is our comfortable reflection that if by struggling we can avoid that servile subjection which Britain demanded, we remain a free and happy people; but if, through the frowns of Providence, we sink in the struggle, we do but remain the wretched people we should have been without the Declaration. Our hearts are full, our hands are full; may God, in whom we trust, support us.

"Judge Paine was a firm believer in the divine origin of the Christian religion. He gave full credence to the scriptures, as a revelation from God, designed to instruct mankind in a knowledge of their duty, and to guide them in the way to eternal happiness." Rev. Charles A. Goodrich *Lives of the Signers to the Declaration of Independence*. New York: William Reed & Co., 1856. Pages 112-119.

Robert Treat Paine to Robert L. Livingston; Jan. 25, 1776

"...May heaven bless you & all yr. Connections & soon grant us a happy meeting"

Elbridge Gerry

Elbridge Gerry, a student at Harvard, went on to become a merchant. In the area of Marblehead, he was elected a member of the General Court in 1773. Gerry was the roommate of Joseph Warren at the time of the battle of Breed's Hill (Bunker Hill). He was on a congressional committee that visited Washington at Valley Forge, which caused better support for the army.

Elbridge Gerry to Joseph Trumbull; Oct. 22, 1776

> "This is a critical Time for our affairs at Ticonderoga as well as New York; may God support & prosper them.

Elbridge Gerry to Joseph Hawley; Jan. 1, 1777

> "... Let us exert Ourselves to these purposes, & in twelve months with the Blessing of God I doubt not We shall see the Independence of America established on a Foundation that cannot be shaken by the Arms of Tyranny.

Elbridge Gerry to James Warren (May 20, 1776) IV, 43.

> "Amidst all our difficulties you would be highly diverted to see the situation of our 'moderate gentlemen.' They have been more apprehensive of evils than any others, as we have frequently observed, and they have now the mortification to find that their measures for avoiding have but served to increase them. I sometimes think that Providence permitted them to clog the affairs of the colonies, that they may become in some degree desperate, and thus introduce into the circle of determined men those timid beings, whose constitution never admits of their defending freedom on the noblest principles, and are afterwards obliges to meet danger by the same motives that induce them to shun it. They are coming over to us, but I am sorry their counter influence so long prevented

us from adopting the only means by which we could supply ourselves with the necessaries for defence."

John Hancock

Most biographies of John Hancock focus on the rich uncle that left John in charge of the lucrative trading business. Not only was John the son of a minister, he was the grandson of one also. Part of the objective for the British forces going to Lexington and Concord was to capture Hancock and Adams. Where were they staying? I would not be surprised if you were never told that he was staying at the house of a relative, Rev. Clarke. He left Rev. Clarke's house and stayed with Rev. Merritt. After staying with Rev. Merritt, he stayed with Rev. Thaddeus Burr in Fairfield, Connecticut. Notice that Hancock was not turned away by either of these ministers. None of the three ministers cried the current garbage of "separation of church and state." "We can't get involved in politics."

John Hancock to George Washington; March 6, 1776

"…By the Perserverance and the Blessing of God, I trust, if we continue to deserve Freedom, we shall be enabled to overcome them. To that Being, in whose hands is the fate of Nations, I recommend you and the Army under your Command."

John Hancock to Dorothy Hancock; March 5, 1777

"…May the Almighty God be your constant protection. Rely on him & he will not forsake you."

John Hancock, Day of Prayer Proclamation, April 15, 1775

"In circumstances dark as these, it becomes us, as Men and Christians, to reflect that, whilst every prudent Measure should be taken to ward off the impending Judgements…All confidence must be withheld from the means we use; and reposed only on that GOD who rules in the Armies of Heaven, and without whose Blessing the best human Counsels are but Foolishness- and all created Power Vanity"

John Hancock to the States (Sept. 24, 1776), V

"...I am persuaded, under the gracious Smiles of Providence, assisted by our most strenuous Endeavours, we shall finally succeed agreeably to our Wishes; and thereby establish the Independence, the Happiness and the Glory of the United States."

Stephen Hopkins

The mother of Stephen Hopkins was the daughter of one of the first Baptist ministers of Providence. He started as a self-taught farmer until 1731 when he started a mercantile business. He was a representative to the General Assembly in 1732 and in 1741 was chosen Speaker of the House of Representatives. In 1751 he was chosen Chief Justice of Rhode Island. He served as governor from 1756 to 1767.

In 1774 he introduced a bill into the Assembly of Rhode Island to prevent the importation of slaves and freed all those which he owned. He attended Friends meetings until his death in 1785.

Stephen Hopkins was on committees for the funerals of Peyton Randolph (Journals of Continental Congress, III, p. 303) and Samuel Ward (Journals of Continental Congress, IV, 237.) The committee was asked by Congress to superintend the funeral and request that a sermon be preached at the service. Listen to Sherman's letter to Henry Ward describe the funeral which Congress had for Henry's brother Samuel (March 27, 1776):

> "His funeral is to be attended, this day at three o'clock, by the Congress as Mourners- by the General Assembly of the Province of Pennsylvania, and the Corporation of the City of Philadelphia-...the Clergy of all denominations preceding the Corpse- Six very respectable Gentlemen of this city being Pallbearers. He will be carried into the Great Presbyterian Meeting house in Arch Street, where a Funeral discourse will be delivered by the revd. Mr. Stillman. The Corpse will from thence be carried to the Baptist burying ground in this city & there interred."

Stephen Hopkins to Ruth Hopkins [daughter-in-law] Nov. 15, 1775

> "I am in very good Health as your Mother also is wishing we might return to you. When that will be only Heaven knows."

His trembling signature shows the onset of paralysis. He had to use his left hand to help him write with his right hand.

William Ellery

At the signing of the Declaration, William Ellery placed himself beside Secretary Charles Thomson so that he could see the faces of the men who were signing their death warrant. He saw faces of patriots who counted the cost and would give their lives if necessary. The British burned Ellery's house. In times of public danger, Ellery would comfort himself and others by this phrase from the Psalms: "The Lord reigneth!"

<u>William Ellery to Ezra Stiles; July 20, 1776</u>

"...The Road to Liberty, like the Road to Heaven is strewed with Thorns. Virtue lives in Exertion. But thank Providence, altho' our Northern Army hath been unsuccessful, our Southern Forces under Gen. Lee have been successful.

<u>William Ellery to Christopher Ellery; Jan. 26, 1778</u>

"...When the war will end I know not; but I hope it will not extend beyond this year at farthest. It will end sooner if the divine Providence should remove from British Councils that infatuation which has so long prevailed in them; but *quo deus vult rius dementent* [Those whom God wishes to destroy he first makes mad.]

<u>William Ellery to William Vernon (March 16, 1778), IX, 302</u>

"...With the aid of Heaven we will crush the Serpents head next Summer, and force our Enemies to be at peace with Us!"

<u>William Ellery to Nicolas Cooke (Dec. 25, 1778) IV, 653</u>

"...I hope in God better Fortune will attend our future Operations."

Roger Sherman

Roger Sherman was the only one of the Founders to sign all four of the major founding documents: the Articles of Association (1774), the Declaration of Independence (1776), the Articles of Confederation (1777) and the Constitution of the United States (1787). Those that say the Founders were deists and atheists walk blindly over graves like Sherman's which reads:

> "He ever adorned the profession of Christianity which he made in his youth; and, distinguished through life for public usefulness, died in the prospect of a blessed immortality."

Roger Sherman's Creed

Roger Sherman revised the wording of a creed for the White Haven Congregational Church in 1788:

> "I believe that there is only one living and true God, existing in three persons, the Father, the Son and the Holy Ghost, the same in substance equal in power and glory. That the scriptures of the old and new testaments are a revelation from God, and a complete rule to direct us how we may glorify and enjoy him."

Please note that a known Christian is on the committee concerning the 1st Amendment.

Samuel Huntington

Samuel Huntington became president of the Continental Congress in 1779 when John Jay left the position to represent the United States in Spain. While president, Huntington called for a day of prayer. The man who called the nation to prayer became chief justice of Connecticut in 1786 and kept that position until his death in 1796.

Samuel Huntington to the Sultan of Morocco, Dec. 1780

"...Signed in, and by Order of Congress of the thirteen United States of North America, Day of Month of December in the year **of our LORD Christ** 1780 and of our Independence 5."

Samuel Huntington to the States, March 21, 1781

"...Your excellency will receive herewith enclosed, a Proclamation of the 20th Instant, earnestly recommending that Thursday the third of May be observed as a Day of Humiliation, Fasting & Prayer by all the United States."

Samuel Huntington to James Cogswell; March 30, 1776

"...On Sunday morning the 17th Inst. my attention from my chamber window was Suddenly called to behold a mighty Calvalcade of Plebians marching thro' the Street with drums beating and at every Small distance they halted & gave three Huzzas. I was apprehensive Some outrage was about to be committed, but Soon perceived my mistaken apprehensions & that it was a Religious exercise of the Sons of Saint Patrick, it being the anniversary of that Saint the morning Exercise was ushered in with the ceremony above described."

Samuel Huntington served on a committee (along with Daniel Roberdeau, and Nathaniel Scudder) "to prepare a recommendation to the United States, to set apart a day of fasting, humiliation and prayer." Journals of Continental Congress, X, 207.

William Williams

William Williams was the son of a minister as well as a grandson of a minister. He was elected as a deacon in his congregational church at a young age. He professed Christ at a relatively young age. He fought in the French and Indian Wars. Get a taste of William's faith in his letter to Jonathan Trumball, Nov.6, 1776:

"Let all Eyes and Hearts be to God...all things are in the hands of our exquisitely wise and good God. May every soul be induced to repent and seek Him with all their heart and entreat his favor for this distressed Land."

If you are dead-set convinced that all the Founders were deists and atheists, please don't read his Sept. 20, 1776 letter to Jonathan Trumbull, Sr. You may say that his grammar needs some improvement, but you cannot say this man was an atheist or a deist.

<u>William Williams to Jonathan Trumbull, Sr., Sept. 20, 1776</u>
"It will undoubtedly be needless for me to give You any account of the Evacuations of N. York by our army on Sab. Day the 15th, of most of our heavy Cannon falling into the hands of our Enemies &c, as it will be communicated to you by my Bror. Commissa., many ways ee'r this can reach your Hand. This Event unhappy & distressing as it is has been forseen & known ever since the quitting of Long Island, & had been determined by the Genl. & his Council; Congress had been made fully acquainted with & assented by the Genl. & assented to it as absolutely necessary, & directed that it shod not be destroyed by Us on leaving it. These Events however, & signal advantage gained by our oppressors, & the Distress to which our Army & Country are & must be subjected in Consequence of them, are loud speaking Testimonies of the Displeasure & Anger of almighty God against a sinful People, louder than sevenfold Thunder. Is it possible that the most obdurate & stupid of the Children of America shod not hear & tremble? God has surely a Controversie with

this People, & He is most certainly able to manage it & He will accomplish his Designs, & bring Us to Repentance & Reformation or destroy Us. We must bend or break. The ways of his Providence are dark & deep bur they are holy, wise & altogether right, tho our feeble Understandings comprehend them not, & tho his Chastisements are severe & dreadful. They are dictated by unbounded Wisdom & Love. They have a meaning of awful & kind Import. Turn unto me for why will ye die O Sons of America? We have thought God was for Us & had given many & signal Instances of his Power & Mercy in our Favor, & had greatly frowned upon & disappointed our Enemies & verily it has been so, but have we repented and given him the glory? Verily no. His hand seems to be turned & stretched out against Us, & strong is his Hand & high is his right Hand. He can & will accomplish all his Pleasure. It is God who has blunted the Weapons of our warfare, that has turned the Counsels of wise Men into foolishness, that has thus far blasted & disappointed our Hopes, & made Us flee before our Enemies, & given them Possession of our Strong Holds. Trouble does not spring out of the dust nor rise out of the Ground. I have always thot this was a just & righteous Cause in which We are engaged. I remain unshaken in that firm persuasion, & that God wod sooner later vindicate & support it, I believe so still, but I believe this People must first be brot to know & Acknowledge the righteousness of his Judgment, & their own exceeding Sinfullness & Guilt, & be deeply humbled under his mighty hand & look & cry & to trust in Him for all their help & Salvation but in the Use & Exertion of all the Strength He has given Us. Surely We have seen enough to convince Us of all this & then why are we not convinced, why is not every Soul humbled under the mighty hand of God, repenting & mourning For its Sin & putting away the evil of his Doings, & looking to Him that smites Us by humble, earnest Prayer & Supplication day & night. Why are not the dear Children of God (surely there are many, who their Sins & back slidings & for all the abominations that are done in the Land, & saying spare, spare thy People O Lord & give not thine Heritage to Reproach. Let not the Vine which thy right Hand has planted here be rooted up & destroyed, let not thy Churches be wasted & devoured, let not virtue & the remains of Religion be torn down & trampled in the Dust, Let not thy Name be blasphemed, not our insulting wicked Foes say where is your God, nor the profane world that there is no God that rules the world & regardeth the Right, that vindicateth the just & the righteous Cause. I know that God can vindicate his own Name & Honor without our Help, & out of the Stones raise up Children to Abraham, & it is amazing Folly & Madness to cry the Temple, the Temple of the Lord, & trust in that while We remain an incorrigible People. But Such Things are what God wod have Us learn & practice while his Judgments fill our Mouths, & pour out our Souls before Him. Are any? Are not all? In New England especially who have any Interest in Heaven, crying, begging & intreating for the pouring of blessed Spirit of God upon the Land, tis a most grievous & distressing Consideration that God is pleased so to withhold the blessed Influence & operations thereof, without which We shall remain stupid forever. Therefore with redoubled fervency of ardent Prayer & Supplication, shod every Soul that has one Sparck of Heavenly Fire kindle it to a fervent Heat & expanded Blaze.

"O New England, O my dear native Land, how does my Soul Love thee. Be instructed therefore lest God's Soul depart from thee, lest thou be like Corazin & Bethsaida in Condemnation as thou hast been in Privileges, lest He make thee as Admah & set thee as Zeboiin. Are the Ministers of the Gospel alive & lifting up their Voices like a trumpet & sounding the Alarm of the Almighty's Anger & Wrath ready to burst on the defenseless Heads of a guilty People? Are they warning the wicked of their infinite Danger, animating & arousing them to Consideration? Are they with ardent Zeal & Fervour animating & enlivening the languid Graces of the Godly, exciting & leading them to fervent Praying, sighing & crying for their own Declensions & Luke warmness in

Religion & for the Sins & Iniquities of the Land, praying, begging & intreating with unceasing & as it were resistless Importunity for the copious Effusions of the Blessed spirit upon all orders & degrees of People & refusing to let God go without an Answer of Peace, & in the midst of Wrath to remember Mercy, & not give up his Heritage to Reproach nor blast the blooming Hopes & Prospects of this infant Country, the Asylum of Liberty & Religion?

"Strange that Mankind should need such alarming Providences to produce such an Effect. It is no more than to act like reasonable Creatures, to possess a Spirit & Temper that will a thousand fold sweetness & pleasure to all the Enjoyments of this World, to exchange the Slavery of the Devil, that accursed Enemy of our Souls, for the Service of God & the Liberty of his Children, to do justly, to love Mercy & walk humbly with our God, to answer the sole end of our Creation, to secure a Peace here infinitely better than the World can give, & an Eternity of Peace & Happiness in the world to come. But still more strange if possible, & astonishing is it that They Shod disregard the Voice of the most high, remain thoughtless & stupid under the dreadful Tokens of his Anger & the awful Judgments of his Hand, by Sickness & by the Sword of our unnatural & enraged Enemies threatening to depopulate the Land & drench the Plains with the Blood of its Inhabitants, leaving the weeping Widows, helpless Orphans & the all that survive the shocking carnage & subsequent Masacre to drag out their Lives in Want, wretchedness & miserable bondage & all this aggravated with the certain Prospect of leaving this dreadful Curse intailed on all Posterity.

"A thorough Repentance & Reformation without all peradventure will appease the Anger of a holy & just God, avert these amazing Calamities, secure Liberty & Happiness to this & all succeeding Ages & Felicity & Glory to all the Subjects of it. If such Considerations & Motives wont awaken a[ll] to serious thoughtfulness & Attention, I know not what will, but the Voice of the Arch Angel & the Trumpet of God.

"P.S. You will not think proper to communicate this Letter to the Assembly. I am anxious beyond the power of Language to describe, of contributing something to the Good & Salvation, temporal & eternal of my Countrymen. (Hope I have not been totally useless here.) If you shod think this may have any tendency to awaken our sleepy People & be of no disadvantage, I am willing it should be printed & for no other possible reason, leaving out such of the beginning as may be a clue to guess the author or where He is, & with the description or Signature of a Letter from a Gent of Connecticut, now in a different colony.

Oliver Wolcott

Oliver Wolcott split his time during the War for Independence between serving in the Continental Congress and Army service. He commanded a brigade of militia, which took part in the defeat of Burgoyne in 1777. Wolcott's Christian faith shines through in his writings. Listen to what he wrote to his wife Laura in April 10, 1776:

"…Merciful Providence still continues my Health to Me. Thro Various Scenes of Life God has sustained Me. May he ever be my unfailing Friend, May his Love cherish my Soul, May my Heart with gratitude Acknowledge his Goodness and may my Desires be to Him and to the remembrance of his Name…may God give us strength to travel the upward Road. May the divine Redeemer conduct us to that Seat of Bliss which he himself has prepared for his Friends, at the approach of which every Sorrow shall Vanish from the human heart, and endless scenes of Glory Open upon the enraptured Eye. There our Love to God and each other will grow stronger, and our Pleasures never be damp'd by the Fear of future Separation."

Oliver Wolcott to Roger Newberry, June 4, 1776

"…I am most sincerely sorry for the distress of my Country but let a man Consider that every thing which he holds dear is at Stake. That a Conquest by our Enemies ensures Slavery and Misery thro endless Generations. Is this a Patrimony which we must leave our Children? God forbid! Not he who sitteth in the Heavens, who holds Empires in his hands, who holds the Tyrant Worms of this earth, in utter division, he will Crush the Power of the Oppresor, he will Vindicate the Cause of the Righteous, he will preserve his People like a Flock, and by the Arm of his Power make them to know their Almighty Deliverer- While the Malice of the Oppressor shall cease and he who fears not the Justice of God shall perish for ever. I firmly believe this Country will be saved. Let us take up the Resolution of Joab, play the Man for the cities of our God; and let God do as it pleases him."

Josiah Bartlett

Josiah Bartlett's ancestors were from Normandy in France. His mother's maiden name was Webster and was a relative of the family of Daniel Webster. When the governor of New Hampshire dissolved the Assembly in 1776, Bartlett was at the head of the Committee of Safety. Bartlett had served under the British governor, Wentworth. When Bartlett became a member of the Continental Congress in 1775, Gov. Wentworth struck his name from the magistracy list. He served from 1787 to 1793 as president of New Hampshire.

Josiah Bartlett to Mary Bartlett, July 14, 1776

> "..But I hope & trust that the Supreme Disposer of all Events, who loveth Justice & hateth Iniquity will continue to favor our righteous Cause and that the wickedness of our Enemies will fall on their own heads."

Josiah Bartlett to Nathaniel Folsom; Sept. 2, 1776

> "…What the congress will do is at present uncertain but hope they will be directed by the Supreme Disposer of Events, to do in this & Every other affair before them what will be most Conducive to the Safety & Happiness of these American States."

Josiah Bartlett to Mary Bartlett; Oct. 11, 1775

> "I can now inform you that by the Goodness of God I am in a Good State of health Tho I have not Quite got my Strength up."

Josiah Bartlett to Nathaniel Folsom; Sept. 2, 1776

> "What the Congress will do is at present uncertain but hope they will be directed by the Supreme Disposer of Events, to do this & Every other affair before them what will be

the most Conducive to the Safety & Happiness of these American States."

<u>Josiah Bartlett signed the Articles of Confederation</u> which stated:

"…Whereas it hath pleased the Great Governor of the World to incline the hearts of the legislatures we respectively represent in congress."

William Whipple

When William Whipple was a young boy, he worked as a cabin boy on a ship. He left the ship work at age 29 when he went into business with his brother in Portsmouth, New Hampshire. He became a leader in the patriotic movement early on. In 1776 he was chosen to be a delegate to the Continental Congress. In 1777 he resigned from the Continental Congress and became a brigadier general of the New Hampshire Militia and fought against Burgoyne. He died in 1785 while being a side judge of the Superior Court of New Hampshire.

William Whipple to Joshua Brackett; April 11, 1776

"...May the Supreme Governour of the Universe Protect & Defend us, Guide our Councils & Prosper our Arms."

William Whipple to Josiah Bartlett; July 27, 1779

"...Remember our cause is more just than the posterity of Jacob was ever engaged in, yet we are told miracles were wraught in favor of that people, notwithstanding which, it seems there [their] own exertions were always essential for their security, let us exert our selves, as we ought & no doubt Heaven will smile on our endeavours and crown them with success."

William Whipple to John Langdon; Nov. 7, 1776

"...May God unite our hearts in all things that tend to the well being of the rising Empire."

William Whipple voted in the affirmative that the House adjourn on Good Friday, 1778, just like it did in 1776 and 1777. Journals of Continental Congress, XIII, p. 409.

Matthew Thornton

Matthew Thornton was born in Ireland and moved with his family when he was 2-3 years old. He studied medicine. He was appointed to be colonel of the New Hampshire Militia by Governor Wentworth. Thornton became president of the provincial government of New Hampshire when Gov. Wentworth abdicated. Thornton was permitted to sign the Declaration of Independence even though he took his seat in November 1776. Thornton was a consistent and zealous Christian. He wrote a book entitled <u>Paradise Lost; or the Origin of Evil, Called Sin.</u>

<u>New Hampshire Delegates to Matthew Thornton; June 20, 1775</u>

"Your favor of the 24th May is now before us, in answer to which can only say we easily Conceive the 'painful sensation' that every man must feel when he sees the unnatural Conflict between Great Britain and these Colonies rising to such a highth. But when we Consider it, not of our own Seeking, drove by the Sons of Tyranny and Oppression, to the Sad Alternative of being made Slaves, or appealing to the Sword in Defense of our Just liberties, cannot but think we shall stand Justified, before God and man, in vigorously seizing the latter...May the great Author of all things Bless and Assist us, is the most ardent prayer of, your Obedient servant.

John Sullivan
John Langdon"

<u>New Hampshire Delegates to Matthew Thornton; Nov. 3, 1775</u>

"We can't help Rejoice to see this as a ground work of our government, and hope by the Blessing of Divine Providence, never to return to our former Despotick State."

Additional Notes on Wythe, Franklin, Rush, Sherman, Sam Adams, John Adams

George Wythe

Let's look again at the man who taught Jefferson, Madison and Marshall. He was a vestryman at Bruton Parish Church starting in 1769. Listen to Wythe's definition of justice:

"For justice is appointed by God, the golden rule of all possible good to his creatures, it must be of all things the dearest to HIMSELF. He, therefore, who knowingly acts against justice is a rebel against God and a premeditated murderer of mankind."

The British governor of Virginia, Lord Dunmore dissolved the House of Burgesses in 1774 because of a Fast Day Resolution. Notice that the British government tried to shut it down but also notice what our known Founders did- they proclaimed a day of prayer and fasting. The Fast Day Resolution was signed by the chairman of the House of Burgesses- George Wythe.

Great Grandfather, George Keith was Bishop of London

Did I mention that his great grandfather, George Keith was Bishop of London in 1700? His grandfather was sent to America as a representative of the Society for the Propagation of the Gospel in 1702. In 1693, George Keith, the great grandfather denounced the institution of slavery, 3 years before the Friends as an organization attacked it. George Wythe's mother Margaret personally instructed her son and taught him Latin and Greek.

Here is what Wythe said concerning his religious life as found in Brown's biography on page 88:

"Why sir as to our religion I have ever considered it as our best and greatest Friend, those glorious views which it gives of our relation to God, and of our destination to Heaven, on the easy terms of a good life, unquestionably furnish the best motives to virtue; the strongest dissausives from vice; and the richest cordial under trouble, thus far I suppose We are all agreed; but not, perhaps, so entirely in another opinion which is that in the sight of God, moral character is the main point. This opinion very clearly taught by reason,... that in the last day, according to our works of love or hatred, of mercy, or of cruelty, we shall sing with the angels or weep with devils;... that God is love- and that in exact proportion as we grow in love, we grow in His likeness, and consequently shall partake of His friendship and felicity forever, while others therefore have been beating their heads, or embittering their hearts with disputes about forms of baptism, and modes of faith, it has always, thank God struck me as my great duty, constantly to think of this- God is love; and he that walketh in love; walketh in God and God in him."

Not a Deist, Just a Firm Supporter of the Disestablishment of the Anglicans

I know you will find this hard to believe but there are people who say that George Wythe, like all the other Founders, was a deist. Blah, blah, blah. Imogene Brown's definitive biography of Wythe says the following:

> "Even during his lifetime, Wythe had been reputed to be a deist. Possibly this reputation was derived from the fact that after the Revolution, Wythe was a firm supporter of the disestablishment of the Anglican church and from the bench Wythe handed down decisions that were instrumental in stripping the church of its glebe holdings."
>
> "Although Wythe was a devout Christian and by no means a deist, he placed little stock in religious rites and rituals and in his later years was contemptuous of organized religion."

In his later years, Wythe took up the study of Hebrew so that he could study the Scriptures better.

Franklin's Address at the Constitutional Convention

"Mr. President:
"The small progress we have made after four or five weeks...is methinks a melancholy proof of the imperfection of the Human Understanding...

"In the beginning of the Contest with Great Britain, when we were sensible of danger, we had daily prayer in this room for Divine protection- Our prayers, Sir, were heard, & they were graciously answered. All of us who were engaged in the struggle must have observed frequent instances of a superintending Providence in our favor.

"To that kind Providence we owe this happy opportunity of consulting in peace on the means of establishing our future national felicity. And have we now forgotten that powerful friend? Or do we imagine we no longer need His assistance?

"I have lived, Sir, a long time, and the longer I live, the more convincing proofs I see of this truth- that God governs in the affairs of men. And if a sparrow cannot fall to the ground without His notice, is it probable that an empire can rise without His aid?

"We have been assured, Sir, in the Sacred Writings, that "except the Lord build the House, they labor in vain that build it." I firmly believe that without his concurring aid we shall succeed in this political building no better than the Builders of Babel: We shall be divided by our own partial local interests, our projects will be confounded, and we ourselves shall become a reproach and bye word to future ages.

"And what is worse, mankind may hereafter from this unfortunate instance, despair of establishing Governments by Human wisdom and leave it to chance, war and conquest.

"I therefore beg leave to move- that henceforth prayers imploring the assistance of Heaven, and its blessing on our deliberations, be held in this Assembly every morning before we proceed to business, and that one or more of the clergy of this city be requested to officiate in that service."

Was Franklin an Antiseptic Secularist?

Was there no place for Franklin to talk about God and matters of religion? One could get that impression by reading many works about Franklin, especially encyclopedia articles. If people take the time to read Franklin's writings on their own, they will find many thought-provoking ideas about God and religion. Does anyone in the twenty-first century even bother reading his maxims and proverbs? Check out these as a sampler from William J. Federer's <u>America's God and Country</u>, p. 244:

- "Freedom is not a gift bestowed upon us by other men but a right that belongs to us by the laws of God and nature."

- "I have never doubted the existence of the Deity, that he made the world, and governed it by His Providence." [is that a slap to the Deist position?]

- "A good conscience is a continual Christmas."

Consider this: as Pennsylvania's governor in 1748, Franklin proposed Pennsylvania's first Fast Day.

Franklin's Friendship with George Whitefield

Many writings try to dismiss Franklin's connections to George Whitefield (if they mention it at all). If he scarcely knew Whitefield, why did he correspond with Whitefield? Why did Franklin build an auditorium for the sole purpose of having George Whitefield preach there when he came to Pennsylvania? After Whitefield came, Franklin donated the auditorium as the first building of the University of Pennsylvania.

Franklin heard one of Whitefield's sermons in person. Ever the scientist, Franklin checked out the number of the crowd (30,000) as well as recording that Whitefield could be heard a mile away.

Listen to Franklin's reflection about the effect of Whitefield's preaching:

"It was wonderful to see the change soon made in the manners of our inhabitants. From being thoughtless or indifferent about religion, it seemed as if all the world were growing religious, so that one could not walk thro' the town in an evening without hearing psalms sung in different families of every street."

Imagine that for a moment: city streets where <u>families</u> were singing psalms at nighttime together. If you have ever walked through a city at night, that scene would be very welcome in our present society. O, God that once woke up our nation in the 1740s, please do it again!

Franklin's Scientific Contributions

If you are ever in the Philadelphia area, check out the Independence Hall area on one day and the next day check out the Franklin Institute. There you can absorb some of Franklin's contributions, especially in the scientific area. The lightning rod, the Franklin stove, the rocking chair, bifocal glasses and the one arm desk chair were some of his inventions. Seeing some of his projects first hand is enlightening. He founded the first public library and also started what is now the University of Pennsylvania. Franklin also founded the Pennsylvania Hospital. Here is what the cornerstone says:

"In the year of Christ 1755... This building, by the bounty of the Government and of many private persons, was piously founded, for the sick and miserable. May the God of mercies bless the undertaking." (Federer, p. 241)

Don't guys like Franklin get it? They are not supposed to mix government and religion. Can you believe they even mention Christ?

Response to Franklin's Call to Prayer

What was the response to Mr. Franklin's call to prayer at the Constitutional Convention? A New Jersey delegate named Jonathan Dayton reported the following:

> "The Doctor sat down; and never did I behold a countenance at once so dignified and <u>delighted</u> as that of Washington at the close of the address; nor were the members of the convention generally less affected. The words of the venerable Franklin fell upon our ears with a weight and authority, even greater that we may suppose an oracle to have had in a Roman senate!" (Federer, p. 249)

James Madison made a motion and Roger Sherman seconded it. Edmund Jennings Randolph went further: a sermon should be preached at the Constitutional Convention on July 4th & thenceforward prayers will be used in the Convention every morning.

Notice that Washington was delighted. Notice also that Madison made the motion to have prayers. Notice that these men did not shout "separation of church and state!" They did not threaten him with a law suit. Such is the contrast between the wisdom of today and that of the Founders.

John and Abigail

This generation would do well to read the letters between John and Abigail Adams (as well as John and Sally Jay) to see a model of a good marriage. Many think of the Founders were prudes. Check out the number of children these guys had. I wonder how that happens! Marriage, as God intends it, is fun!

The love relationship between John and Abigail is worth your investment in time. Through many hard times, their love stayed firm. Abigail was such a helper for John. What would he have been without her?

John to Abigail, Dec. 3, 1775

"...I hope I shall be excused from coming to Philadelphia again, at least until some other Gentlemen have their turns. But I will never come here without you, if I can persuade you to come with me. Whom God has joined together ought not to be put asunder so long with their consent."

John to Abigail, May 22, 1776

"Among all the Disappointments, and Perplexities, which have fallen to my share in Life, nothing has contributed so much to support my Mind, as the choice Blessing of a Wife, whose capacity enabled her to approve the views of her Husband. This has been the cheering Consolation of my Heart, in my disconsolate Hours. In this remote Situation, I am deprived in a great Measure of this Comfort. Yet I read, and read again your charming letters, and they serve me in some faint degree as a substitute for the company and conversation of the Writer.

"I want to take a walk with you in the Garden- to go over to the Common- the Plain- the Meadow. I want to take Charles in one hand and Tom in the other and walk with you, Nabby on your Right Hand and John upon my left, to view the Corn Fields, the orchards, &c."

John to Abigail, Aug. 10, 1776

"...At the same Time that I am in a State of suspence, Uncertainty and Anxiety about my Best, dearest, worthiest, wisest Friend in this World and all my Children, I am in a State of equal Suspence, Uncertainty, and Anxiety about our Army at New York and Ticonderoga, and consequently about our country and Posterity. The Lives of thousands, and the liberties of Millions are as much in Suspence as the Health of my family. But I submit to the Governance of infinite Wisdom."

John Adams on Rearing Children

John to Abigail, Apr. 15, 1776

"John has genius and so has Charles. Take care they don't go astray. Cultivate their Minds, inspire their little Hearts, raise their Wishes. Fix their Attention upon great and glorious Objects, root out every little Thing, weed out every Meanness, make them great and manly. Teach them to scorn Injustice, Ingratitude, Cowardice and Falsehood. Let them revere nothing but Religion, Morality and Liberty."

John to John Quincy, Apr. 18, 1776

"...I hope you and your Sister and Brothers will take proper notice of these great Events, and remember under whose wise and kind Providence they are all conducted. Not a sparrow falls, nor a Hair is lost, but by the Direction of infinite Wisdom. Much less are cities conquered and evacuated. I hope that you will all remember how many Losses, Dangers and Inconveniences have been born by your Parents, and the Inhabitants of Boston in general for the sake of preserving Freedom for you and yours- and I hope you all will follow the virtuous Example if, in any future Time, your Country's

Liberties should be in Danger, and suffer every human Evil, rather than give them up.

John Adams to Abigail Adams, October 29,1775

"...My opinion of the Duties of Religion and Morality, comprehends a very extensive connection with society at large, and the great Interest of the public. Does not natural Morality, and much more Christian benevolence, make it our indispensible Duty to lay ourselves out to serve our fellow Creatures to the Utmost of our Power, in promoting and supporting those Political systems, and general Regulations upon which the Happiness of Multitudes depends. The Benevolence, Charity, Capacity and Industry which exerted in private Life, would make a family, a Parish or a Town happy, employed upon a larger Scale, in support of the great Principles of Virtue and Freedom of political Regulations might secure whole nations and Generations from Misery, Want and Contempt. Public Virtues, and political Qualities therefore should be incessantly cherished in our Children."

John Adams' Christian Quotes

John to Abigail, June 17, 1775

"Congress chose George Washington to be General of the American Army... We have appointed a continental Fast. Millions will be upon their Knees at once before their great Creator, imploring his Forgiveness and Blessing, his Smiles on American Councils and Arms."

John to Abigail, Oct. 1, 1775

"It may amuse you to hear a Story. A few days ago in company with Dr. Zubly somebody said, there was nobody on our side but the Almighty. The Dr. who is a native of

Switzerland, and speaks but broken English, quickly replied, 'Dat is enough.'"

John to Abigail, June 2, 1775

"Poor Bostonians! My Heart Bleeds for them, day and night. God preserve and bless them."

John Adams to James Warren; Apr. 22, 1777

"The management of so complicated and mighty a Machine as the United Colonies, requires the Meekness of Moses, the Patience of Job and the Wisdom of Solomon added to the Valour of Daniel."

John to Abigail, April 27, 1777

"If there is a moral Law; if there is a divine Law- and that there is, every intelligent Creature is conscious- to trample on these laws, to hold them in Contempt and Defyance; is the highest Exertion of Wickedness, and Impiety, that Morals can be guilty of. The Author of human Nature, who gave it its Rights, will not see it ruined, and suffer its destroyers to take the Alberts, the Phillips, and the Georges- the Alvas, the Grislers and Howes, and vindicate the Wrongs of oppressed human Nature."

John Adams to Abigail Adams, April 15, 1776,

"...But I will not bear the Reproaches of my Children. I will tell them that I studied and laboured to procure a free Constitution of Government for them to solace themselves under, and if they do not prefer this to ample Fortune, to Ease and Elegance, they are not my Children, and I care not what becomes of them...Teach them to scorn Injustice, Ingratitude, Cowardice, and Falsehood. Let them revere nothing but Religion, Morality and Liberty."

Deists and Atheists Refuted by Father (Samuel Adams)

What would the father of the American Revolution say to the contention that the Founders were deists and atheists?

"If this city [Philadelphia] should be surrendered, I should by no means despair of our Cause. It is a righteous Cause and I am fully persuaded righteous Heaven will succeed it. Congress will adjourn to Baltimore in Maryland, about 120 miles from this place, when Necessity requires it and not before. It is agreed to appoint a Day of Prayer & a Committee will bring in a Resolution for that purpose This day. I wish we were a more religious People. That Heaven may bless you here & hereafter is the most ardent Prayer of, my dear, most cordially yours."
(Samuel Adams to Elizabeth Adams; Dec. 11, 1776)

The Father of the American Revolution was fully confident that even if the capital, Philadelphia, was surrendered [and it was]; Adams believed that righteous Heaven would succeed it. The Father also was for a day of prayer. On top of that, he says that he wishes that we were a _more_ religious people. Again, Samuel Adams wanted more, not less religion. Imagine that as a beer commercial.

Samuel Adams- More Than Beer

To the present generation, the name Samuel Adams is the name of a beer, which consumed in large quantities will make you drunk at weekend parties. Listen to Samuel Adams letter to Joseph Warren describing the first meeting of the Continental Congress (Sept. 9, 1774):

"After setting the mode of voting, which is by giving each colony an equal voice, it was agreed to open the Business with Prayer. As many of our warmest Friends are Members of the Church of England, I thought it prudent as well on that as on some other Accounts to move that the Service should be performed by a Clergyman of that Denomination. Accordingly the Lessons of the Day and Prayer were read by the Reverend Mr. Duche, who afterwards made a most excellent extemporary Prayer, by which he discovered himself to be a Gentleman of Sense and Piety, and a warm Advocate for the religious and civil rights of America."

So, you're telling me that the Samuel Adams beer guy was some sort of religious guy?
Yes, his religious beliefs caused him to make a stand for the civil and religious freedom of America. This religious guy was called the Father of the American Revolution.

Samuel Adams Quotations

Let's hear more from the organizer or father of the American Revolution, Samuel Adams.

May 19, 1775

"It is upon the blessing of God alone that we must depend for a happy Issue to our virtuous Struggle."

July 4, 1776

"This day, I trust, the reign of political Protestantism will commence."

Dec. 26, 1776

"The name of the Lord, says the Scripture is a strong Tower, thither the Righteous flee and are safe. Let us secure his Favor, and he will lead us through the Journey of this Life and at length receive us to a better.

April 17, 1777

"I have always been of the opinion, that we must depend upon our own Efforts, under God for the Establishment of our Liberties."

Quotes from a secular source would have quoted that as follows:

"I have always been of the opinion, that we must depend upon our own Efforts….." They would expect you not to dig any deeper and accept it as that. However the quote goes further to say "our own efforts <u>under God".</u>

I think the father of the American Revolution would have a lot to say on the debate about using the term "under God". He himself used it!

under God

Sherman's Christian Stances

Let's document some of Roger Sherman's Christian stances. When Benjamin Franklin (at the Constitutional Convention) requested that Congress be opened every day with prayer, Sherman seconded the motion. Sherman, a known Christian, was on the committee which decided the wording of the First Amendment. The same Sherman urged President George Washington to declare a national day Thanksgiving Day. Sherman objected to a report from the War Committee that would have allowed the army to give 500 lashes to a soldier. Sherman knew his Old Testament well enough to know that the Jews should not give more than 40 lashes (Deuteronomy 25:3).

Roger Sherman- Jonathan Edward's Deacon

Roger Sherman gives us a direct connection between Jonathan Edwards and the Founding Fathers. In 1742 he was a deacon under Jonathan Edward's ministry. We will hear more about Jonathan Edwards but suffice it to say for now that God used him and others to bring about a revival called the Great Awakening. People and communities had a deep sense of the presence of God.

Was Sherman an atheist or a deist? Check out Mr. Sherman for yourself. For Sherman, God was an active part of his life.

In February, 1776 instructions were given to a committee headed for Canada. The Committee consisted of Charles Carroll, Samuel Chase (Maryland), Benjamin Franklin and Bishop John Carroll. (from a letter of John Adams to James Warren, Feb. 18, 1776)

Three people (John Adams, George Wythe and Roger Sherman) were in charge of writing instructions for the committee to follow. Here is one of the requirements:

"All civil rights and the right to hold office were to be extended to persons of any Christian denomination."

Trashing of George Washington

The day has come when George Washington has lost a lot of appeal to Americans. We no longer celebrate his birthday- it's conglomerated into a Presidents' Day. Some history textbooks actually give more space to Marilyn Monroe than they do to some old dude with white hair on the dollar bill. Schools named George Washington have replaced the name with the newest politically correct person. It is okay to name something new after somebody else- just don't relegate George to a minor historical role.

George was not perfect. Since the 1960s, the focus is on two issues: his alleged fling with Sally Fairfax and the fact that he had slaves. Concerning the Sally Fairfax issue, from the evidence I have seen, George is guilty of writing letters. Having read other Founders, there are many people in that time period who wrote to married women. John Adams to Mercy Warren, Thomas Jefferson to Abigail Adams, John Jay to Elizabeth Hamilton, Benjamin Franklin to Sally Jay are examples of men writing to married women with no intent of wrong-doing.

David Barton's article "The Founding Fathers and Slavery" addresses that issue quite well and I recommend his website as it touches on that issue as well as African-American history.

Where would we be without George's contribution to the country? From Brooklyn to Valley Forge to crossing the Delaware to Monmouth to Yorktown, he stood in the gap. God used him.

Bullet-Proof George Washington

On July 9, 1755, George Washington fought at the Battle of the Monongahela against French and Indian forces. Gen. Braddock and all 20 British officers on horseback were killed except for Washington who led the retreat.

George Washington to John A. Washington; July 18, 1755

> "But by the all-powerful dispensations of Providence I have been protected beyond all human probability or expectation;

for I had four bullets through my coat, and two horses shot under me, yet escaped unhurt, although death was leveling my companions on every side of me!"

Chief Red Hawk

In 1770 (15 years after the Battle of the Monogahela) Washington, with a childhood friend named Dr. Craik, revisited the battlefield. Washington met an old Indian chief there.

"I am a chief and ruler over my tribes. My influence extends to the waters of the great lakes and to the far blue mountains.

"I have traveled a long and weary path that I might see the young warrior of the great battle. It was on the day when the white man's blood mixed with the streams of our forests that I first beheld this chief [Washington].

"I called to my young men and said, mark yon tall and daring warrior? He is not of the red-coat tribe- he hath an Indian's wisdom, and his warriors fight as we do- himself alone exposed.

"Quick, let your aim be certain, and he dies. Our rifles were leveled, rifles which, but for you, knew not how to miss- 'twas all in vain, a power mightier far than we, shielded you.

"Seeing you were under the special guardianship of the Great Spirit, we immediately ceased to fire at you. I am old and soon shall be gathered to the great council fire of my fathers in the land of the shades, but ere I go, there is something bids me speak in the voice of the prophecy:

"Listen! The Great Spirit protects that man [pointing at Washington] and guides his destinies- he will become the chief of nations, and a people yet unborn will hail him as the founder of a mighty empire. I am come to pay homage to the man who is the particular favorite of Heaven, and who can never die in battle."

Red Hawk personally shot at Washington 11 times without success.

(David Barton's book <u>The Bullet-Proof George Washington</u>)

Providential Help for Washington

Peter Marshall Jr. and David Manuel in <u>The Light and the Glory</u> give an excellent description about God's hand on George Washington and the Continental Army. In the Battle of Brooklyn, we were outnumbered 8,000 to 30,000. We were outclassed, out armed; you name it, we did not stand a chance. It was the end of August 1776 and the British came calling on New York. It is hard for us to imagine Brooklyn as a battlefield- we usually think of Valley Forge or Yorktown or Gettysburg, etc. as battlefields, but not Brooklyn. Well, 250 Maryland and 250 Delaware soldiers gave up their lives so that the Continental Army could escape. They made several charges against larger numbers to give the army time. You hardly ever hear about their sacrifice.

For two days afterwards, there was a strong storm so that the British did not end the business. On August 30, Washington gave the order to evacuate across the Long Island Sound (known for many shipping accidents). With all the weight of the men and arms, the storm would have done them in at sea. However, the storm stopped and the wind and sea grew calm. At dawn about one-third of the army was still on Long Island. A heavy fog came up and stayed until Washington left on the last boat. Please read Peter Marshall's <u>The Light and the Glory</u> to read about it in detail. It speaks loudly of God's provision and Washington's leadership.

George Washington- Surveyor and Scout

If you would like to do some reading on George Washington, here are some resources: <u>Bullet-Proof George Washington</u> by David Barton and the writings of George Washington himself. Washington's early life makes for some fascinating reading. As a scout and surveyor, he had some adventures. His Dec. 23, 1753 entry tells of his travels out west where he and others went through snow until the horses became too tired to carry them. He and a Mr. Gist went on foot and were shot at and missed at the range of 15 steps by a party of French Indians. They made it to a river where the river had ice on the shores but had about 50 yards of flowing water. They spent a day making a raft. As they crossed, they hit a jam and Washington fell into 10 feet of cold water. How they survived is a miracle.

Sally Fairfax

Two generations have been brought up thinking that George Washington had an affair with Sally Fairfax. This was popularized by James Thomas Flexner and others when they yank the following out of context:

> "None of which events, however, nor all of them together, have been able to eradicate from my mind the recollection of those happy moments, the happiest in my life, which I have enjoyed in your company."

Now for the rest of the story... When Washington was fifteen years old, he started making frequent visits to William Fairfax, Jr. A strong friendship grew between the older Fairfax and young Washington. Keep in mind that George's father died and William Fairfax took George under his wing. They went hunting together many times. The friendship was between William and George. When William married Sarah, the strong friendship that George and William had was extended to include Sally. The letter in question was sent in 1798. Washington had sent William a similar letter describing how the Fairfax estate gave George good youthful memories. George had seen "Belvoir" burned to ruins. He had written to William to try to encourage him over his loss and was likewise trying to comfort Sally after William had died. When read in its entire context, this fabrication is really contorted and cruel to the memory of all involved. I fear for such a revision of any letters I may have sent to people encouraging them in Christ. The Lord only knows how they will be misconstrued.

Washington's Prayer Book

Sunday Morning

Let my heart therefore gracious God be so affected with the glory and majesty of it, that I may not do mine own works but wait on Thee and discharge those weighty duties Thou required of me:

And since Thou art a God of pure eyes, and will be sanctified in all who draw nearer to Thee, who dost not regard the sacrifice of fools, nor hear sinners who tread in Thy courts, pardon I beseech Thee, my sins, remove them from my presence, as far as the east is from the west, and accept of me for the merits of Thy son Jesus Christ.

...so give me peace to hear the calling on me in Thy word, that it may be wisdom, righteousness, reconciliation and peace to the saving of my soul in the day of the Lord Jesus...

Bless my family, kindred, friends and country, be our God and guide this day and forever for His sake, who lay down in the grave and arose again for us, Jesus Christ our Lord, Amen.

Sunday Evening

"...increase my faith, and direct me to the true object, Jesus Christ the Way, the Truth and the Life, bless o Lord, all the people of this land, from the highest to the lowest, particularly those whom Thou hast appointed to rule us in church & state.

"Continue Thy goodness to me this night. These weak petitions I humbly implore Thee to hear, accept and answer for the sake of Thy Dear Son, Jesus Christ our Lord, Amen."

Monday Evening

"...Bless O Lord the whole race of mankind, and let the world be filled with the knowledge of Thee and Thy Son, Jesus Christ."

Tuesday Evening

"...and so into Thy hands I commend myself, both soul and body, in the name of Thy son, Jesus Christ, beseeching Thee, when this life shall end, I may take my everlasting rest with Thee in Thy heavenly kingdom."

Testimony of Others About Washington's Christian Character

Henry Muhlenberg:

"I heard a fine example today, namely that His Excellency General Washington rode around among his army yesterday and admonished each and every one to fear God, to put away the wickedness that has set in and becomes so general, and to practice the Christian virtues. From all appearances, this gentleman does not belong to the so-called world of society, for he respects God Word, believes in the atonement through Christ, and bears himself in humility and gentleness. Therefore, the Lord God has also singularly, yea marvelously, preserved him from harm in the midst of countless perils, ambuscades, fatigue, etc. and has hitherto graciously held him in His hand as a chosen vessel."

<u>Isaac Potts</u>: (a Quaker who was the landlord for Washington while at Valley Forge in response to seeing Washington kneeling in prayer in a woods near headquarters. His wife noticed that something was the matter with him.)

"...If I appear agitated 'tis no more than what I am. I have seen this day what I shall never forget. Till now I have thought that a Christian and a soldier were characters incompatible; but if George Washington be not a man of God, I am mistaken, and still more I shall I be disappointed if God does not through him perform some great thing for this country.

John Marshall:

"Without making ostentatious professions of religion, he was a sincere believer in the Christian faith, and a truly devout man."

Patrick Henry

With Patrick Henry, it's almost comical to see how his references to God are edited out. The anti-God Gestapo goes to great lengths to weed the references to God out of his speech (lest any child should hear such things).

"Is life so dear, or peace so sweet as to be purchased at the price of chains and slavery? ... I know not what course others may take, but as for me, give me liberty or give me death!" That was the public school textbook version. Did they omit anything? "<u>Forbid it Almighty God" was omitted</u>. Check your textbook to see if the editors are part of the Get Rid of God Campaign.

Also take note of Henry's other references to God in his speech. "An appeal to arms and the God of Hosts is all that is left us!" "Sir, we are not weak, if we make a proper use of the means which the God of nature hath place in our power. Three millions of people, armed in the holy cause of liberty, and in such a country as that which we possess, are invincible by any force which our enemy can send against us. Besides, sir, we shall not fight out battles alone." "There is a just God who presides over the destinies of nations, and who will raise friends to fight our battles for us."

When Patrick was twelve years old, his mother became a member in Samuel Davies's church. Here again is yet another link from the Great Awakening to the Founding Fathers. Patrick claimed that Davies was the greatest orator he ever heard.

Patrick Henry became Virginia's first governor on July 5, 1776. He held that position for three years.

> "This is all the inheritance I can give to my dear family. The religion of Christ can give them one which will make them rich indeed." <u>The Last Will and Testament of Patrick Henry</u>

"Give Me Liberty or Give Me Death" Patrick Henry

"...There is no longer any room for hope. If we wish to be free- if we mean to preserve inviolate those inestimable privileges for which we have been contending- if we mean not basely to abandon the noble struggle in which we have so long been engaged, and which we pledged ourselves never to abandon until the glorious object of our contest shall be obtained, we must fight! I repeat it, sir, we must fight! An appeal to arms and the God of Hosts is all that is left us!

"They tell us, sir, that we are weak, unable to cope with so formidable an adversary. But when shall we be stronger? Will it be next week, or the next year? Will it be when we are totally disarmed, and when a British guard shall be stationed in every house? Shall we gather strength by irresolution and inaction? Shall we acquire the means of effectual resistance by lying supinely on our backs and hugging the delusive phantom of hope, until our enemies shall have bound us hand and foot? Sir, we are not weak, if we make a proper use of the means which the God of nature hath place in our power. Three millions of people, armed in the holy cause of liberty, and in such a country as that which we possess, are invincible by any force which our enemy can send against us. Besides, sir, we shall not fight out battles alone. There is a just God who presides over the destinies of nations, and who will raise friends to fight our battles for us. The battle, sir, is not to the strong alone; it is to the vigilant, the active, the brave. Besides, sir we have no election. If we were base enough to desire it, it is too late to retire from the contest. There is no retreat but in submission and slavery! Our chains are forged! Their clanking may be heard on the plains of Boston! The war is inevitable- and let it come! I repeat it, sir, let it come!

"It is in vain, sir, to extenuate the matter. Gentlemen may cry, peace, peace! but there is no peace. The war is actually begun! The next gale that sweeps from the north will bring to our ears the clash of resounding arms! Our brethren are already in the field! Why stand we here idle? What is it that gentlemen wish? What would they have? Is life so dear, or peace so sweet, as to be purchased at the price of chains and slavery? Forbid it Almighty God! I know not what course others may take, but as for me: Give me liberty or give me death!"

The following is a story about the weight of a man with integrity. In 1781, British general Cornwallis sent troops to attack Charlottesville to capture Governor Jefferson and the General Assembly.

"It is said that as Patrick Henry, Benjamin Harrison, Judge Tyler and Colonel Christian were hurrying along, they saw a little hut in the forest. An old woman was chopping wood by the door. The men were hungry, and stopped to ask her for food.
"Who are you?" she asked.
"We are members of the legislature, said Patrick Henry; "we have just been compelled to leave Charlottesville on account of the British."
"Ride on, then, ye cowardly knaves!" she said in wrath. "Here are my husband and sons just gone to Charlottesville to fight for ye, and you running away with all your might. Clear out! Ye shall have nothing here."
"But," replied Mr. Henry, "we were obliged to flee. It would not do for the legislature to be broken up by the enemy. Here is Mr. Benjamin Harrison; you don't think he would have fled had it not been necessary?"
"I always thought a great deal of Mr. Harrison till now," answered the old woman, "but he'd no business to run from the enemy." And she started to shut the door in their faces."
"Wait a moment, my good woman, cried Mr. Henry; "would you believe that Judge Tyler or Colonel Christian would take to flight if there were not good cause for so doing?"
"No, indeed that I wouldn't."
"But," he said, "Judge Tyler and Colonel Christian are here."
"They are? Well, I would never have thought it. I didn't suppose they would ever run from the British; but since they

have, they shall have nothing to eat in my house. You may ride along."

Things were getting desperate. Then Judge Tyler stepped forward: "What would you say, my good woman, if I were to tell you that Patrick Henry fled with the rest of us?"

"Patrick Henry!" she answered angrily, "I should tell you there wasn't a word of truth in it! Patrick Henry would never do such a cowardly thing."

"But this is Patrick Henry," said Judge Tyler.

The old woman was astonished; but she stammered and pulled at her apron string, and said: "Well, if that's Patrick Henry, it must be all right. Come in, and ye shall have the best I have in the house."

Mark Beliles and Stephen McDowell. <u>In God We Trust</u>, pp. 164-5.

John Dickinson

"The penman of the American Revolution" never signed the Declaration of Independence. As a matter of fact, he voted against it. Most discussions about Dickinson leave it at that. The rest of the story is that he fought for the Delaware militia. He represented Delaware in the Continental Congress in 1779. He was president of Delaware in 1781 and Pennsylvania in 1782.

Before the Revolution, Dickinson wrote a series of letters entitled "Letters From a Farmer in Pennsylvania." He enumerated the colonists' grievances against unjust British policies.

Coming from a Quaker background, he was opposed to the violence part. However, take note that he and many other Quakers joined the Revolutionary cause (see the Joseph Hewes article), including Gen. Greene. John Dickinson was one of the authors of "A Declaration of the Necessity of Taking Up Arms" in 1775.

David McCullough, the writer of "John Adams" conveys the sense of Dickinson when he has Dickinson lead the militia outside Independence Hall at the first public reading of the Declaration of Independence.

John was born in Trappe, Maryland. He went to school in Philadelphia and England. His plantation outside Dover, Delaware is a "must see" stop for families going through that area.

John Dickinson's Draft Address to the King, Oct. 22, 1774

"Had Almighty God been pleased to give us our Existence in a Land of Slavery, the Sense of our Condition might have been mitigated by the Force of Education & Habit. But Thanks be to his adorable Goodness, we were born Heirs of Freedom, and ever enjoyed our Right under the Auspices of your Royal Ancestors, whose Family was seated on the British Throne, to secure a pious & gallant Nation from the Popery and Despotism, meditated by a superstitious, and inexorable Tyrant...We doubt not, but your royal Wisdom must approve the Sensibility, that teaches your subjects anxiously to guard the Blessing they received from Divine

Providence and thereby to prove the performance of that Compact, that elevated the illustrious House of Brunswick to the Dignity it now possesses...

"Permit Us then, Gracious Sovereign, in the Name of all your faithful People in America, with the utmost Humility to implore You, for the Honor of Almighty God, whose pure Religion our Enemies are undermining..."

Alexander Hamilton

It has been stated earlier that the Founding Fathers were not perfect. Alexander Hamilton shows how greatness can be flawed, humbled and then redeemed. Christopher Yates sums it up well in the title of his book, <u>Alexander Hamilton: How the Mighty Are Redeemed.</u>

Through no fault of his own, Alexander started life being an illegitimate son in the West Indies. His mother was Rachel Faucett (who was from French Huguenot background). Her family gave her to be married to an older man, John Lavier on the island of St. Croix while she was a teenager. John had her imprisoned and when she got out of prison she went back to Nevis Island where she came from. She had a fifteen year romance with James Hamilton and had two children by him, James Jr., and then Alexander in 1755 or 1757. John Lavier had divorced her in the meantime. When James Hamilton moved to St. Croix, there was quite a fuss made concerning Rachel. She was accused of being an adulteress and under Danish law she could not remarry. James got tired of fighting the hastle and abandoned Rachel and the two boys.

That was hardly an easy circumstance to be born into. He eventually found work in Christiansted as a clerk for Nicolas Kruger. He wrote correspondence letters for Kruger and even had an article printed in the local paper concerning a hurricane when he was fifteen. Hugh Knox, a minister (educated at the College of New Jersey-which later was called Princeton) arrived in 1772 and became his tutor. When Alexander finished his tutoring, Kruger allowed him to go to New York in hopes of studying at Princeton. William Livingston (John Jay's father-in-law as well as the governor of New Jersey) and Elias Boudinot (later the President of the Continental Congress and the first President of the American Bible Society) were Hamilton's advisors. Hamilton first met Jay at Liberty Hall, where William Livingston lived. It was in this 1772-74 time period that Jay was courting and eventually married Livingston's daughter, Sarah (Sally). Hamilton wanted to graduate as soon as possible from Princeton, take more than a full load and finish sooner than others would. He interviewed with John Witherspoon but was not allowed to do such a program. A fellow named James Madison had finished in two years. That sounds nice but he suffered a nervous collapse afterwards. Witherspoon did not want that happening to another student. Hamilton ended up attending King's College (where Jay graduated).

Robert Troup was Alexander's roommate at King's. After Hamilton's death, Robert wrote about Alexander's prayer life. He had a habit of praying on his knees for morning and evening prayers. Troup said that he had been affected by Hamilton's fervor and eloquence in prayer.

The Boston Tea Party happened two months after he started his studies at King's. It is always difficult going to college in the midst of a war and it was so for Hamilton. He wrote two pamphlets "A Full Vindication of the Measures of Congress," and "The Farmer Refuted." He wrote so well that people thought that Jay had written the pamphlets.

By March 1776 he was captain of an artillery company and later became General George Washington's aide. Troup visited Hamilton while he was the captain of the artillery and made note of Hamilton's continued habit of prayer.

Alexander met and married Elizabeth Schuyler in Albany, New York in December, 1780. Elizabeth was the daughter of General Philip Schuyler. Alexander resigned as Washington's aide in April 1781. Colonel Hamilton was in Yorktown, Virginia and led the charge on the redoubts.

After Yorktown, Hamilton served as a delegate to the Continental Congress (1782). He also helped create the New York Society for Promoting the Manumission of Slaves.

When the Congress was working on the Constitution, Hamilton worked with James Madison and John Jay by writing what are called the Federalist Papers. This present writer would encourage you to read them for yourself. I personally come from generations of Democrats and the Federalist Papers started me thinking about being a Republican. Their concept of the flawed nature of mankind and the need for checks and balances hit a resonating chord with me.

Here comes the car wreck! In 1791 a woman named Maria Reynolds came to his door asking for help. She had been abandoned by her husband, James Reynolds and had a five year old son. Hamilton gave into temptation and committed adultery with her. The husband used this situation to extort money from Hamilton. Charges were leveled against Hamilton in the government that he was using government money to pay off the Reynolds. In 1797, Hamilton confessed to his sin. He put the interests of the new nation above that of his own. He wrote a pamphlet saying that he took no government money but that he indeed had sinned by having an affair with Mrs. Reynolds. He left government work after that.

Hamilton was very disturbed by the atheistic engine that was running France. Their revolution was of a different sort than the American one. The American Revolution came as a last resort. Many pleas, remonstrances were sent to the king. Many turned after seeing the events of Lexington and Concord- we had to defend ourselves or be crushed. As this book demonstrates, the American Founders had a deep faith in God and had a specific Christian worldview. The French Revolution was of a different nature. God's word was not the basis for their law- the word of the mob was. This is what the Federalist Papers had warned about. Hamilton, Madison and Jay had warned about mob rule.

In a series of articles called "The Stand," Hamilton was upset with the rise of godlessness in America which was mostly due to the popularity of the French Revolution. Remember the illustration stated earlier about how the nation Israel turned away from God in one generation. After Joshua died, the people turned away from God. America was going through the same thing. In 1796, only twenty years after the signing of the Declaration of Independence, only one member of the Yale graduates claimed to believe in God. History repeats itself because the human heart is the same. Hamilton wrote in "The Stand":

> "The open profession of Atheism in the Convention, received with acclamations; the honorable mention on its journals of a book professing to prove the nothingness of all religion; the institution of a festival to offer public worship to a cortezan decorated with the pompous [title] of 'Goddess of Reason': the congratulatory reception of impious children appearing

in the hall of the Convention to lisp blasphemy against the King of Kings; are among the dreadful proofs of a conspiracy to establish Atheism on the ruins of Christianity- to deprive mankind of its best consolations and most animating hopes- and to make a gloomy desert of the universe."

Along with the French Atheism, Thomas Paine's book <u>The Age of Reason</u> was becoming popular. People who followed the French ideals were called Francophiles. Thomas Jefferson and Thomas Paine were seen by people as a threat to the new nation (by Federalists such as Hamilton). Can you see how the temptation that Hamilton succumbed to diminished his moral authority to speak on the issues? Be that as it may, Hamilton tried to oppose the atheistic ideas. In a April 1802 letter to a James Bayard (from Delaware), Hamilton suggested the start of a Christian Constitutional Society.

Hamilton felt the sting of being called a bastard in his early youth and took the sting of being an adulterer. He was a Christian. He repented of his sin. God forgave him. But how much better he and his family would have been if he had fled from temptation!

Aaron Burr was vice president under Jefferson. He almost made it to president but Hamilton blocked his way. Hamilton chose Jefferson as the lesser of two evils. We talked earlier about links with the Great Awakening. Aaron Burr's grandfather was Jonathan Edwards. Burr was raised by Jonathan Edwards, Jr., his uncle. Burr himself went to Princeton and studied under John Witherspoon. When Burr tried to run for governor in New York, Hamilton made sure behind the scenes that Burr did not win. Burr and Hamilton exchanged letters and a duel was decided upon. Burr shot Hamilton and he died of his wounds. Before dying, Hamilton received communion from Rev. Benjamin Moore. He reaffirmed "a strong confidence in the mercy of God through the intercession of the Redeemer."

Hamilton's life is a hard lesson even to us today. What a climb to power from such poor beginnings! What a fall from power when one gives in to lusts of the flesh! What a Redeemer that pardons!

John Jay

What would you think of a president who nominated someone to the Supreme Court who was a known evangelical Christian? Would the Founding Fathers have voted down someone who mentioned God and having faith in God 33 times in a public address? Would the Founders be shocked if that person became president of the American Bible Society?

Most people think of the Founders as being only English. Jay was from French Huguenot background (as were Elias Boudinot, Alexander Hamilton, Paul Revere, Henry Laurens and Francis Marion the Swamp Fox). He graduated from King's College in 1764 and was there when Samuel Johnson was president (Anglican minister in the Great Awakening). King's College had morning and evening prayers. It is difficult to imagine in today's university climate but in the universities of the American Revolution era, students prayed and God was an integral part of the classroom.

John was Anglican and tended toward keeping ties with England. He met Sarah (Sally) Livingston in 1772 and married her in 1774. Her father, William Livingston, was a strong Presbyterian (attended Rev. James Caldwell's church in Elizabethtown, New Jersey). He attended the first Continental Congress in 1774 along with his new father-in-law. Jay was not present at the signing of the Declaration of Independence because the New York Assembly forbade him to go. The British fleet had left Boston and they knew New York was next. The British attacked New York in late August.

Jay served as Chief Justice of the state of New York and then became President of the Continental Congress from 1778 to October 1779. He left because he was commissioned Minister Plenipotentiary to Spain, which meant he was sent as the minister authorized to attempt to obtain help from Spain. His wife Sally accompanied him on the trip. If they were caught by a British ship, certain peril awaited them. They were in a storm for about two weeks. The three masts were broken and the rudder was damaged. Being in a storm for two weeks in the middle of the Atlantic Ocean tends to show how one stands with the Lord. There was no 911 number to call-the whole matter is between you and God. After they arrived in

Martinique (where they boarded another ship), Sally wrote to her mother describing Jay's character. The Spain mission was basically a failure but Jay learned some key negotiating skills while there which helped when he, Franklin and John Adams negotiated the Treaty of Paris (1783).

He became the Secretary of Foreign Affairs (while the government was still under the Articles of Confederation) when he returned to the United States. He helped Hamilton and Madison write the Federalist Papers but only wrote five articles. He would have written more but he was hit on the head with a brick and almost died. Apparently, some children had spread rumors about a doctor throwing amputated arms out of a window. A mob came and was about to kill the doctor when Jay confronted the mob.

Jay was chosen by George Washington to be the first Chief Justice under the new Constitution. In 1789 the Federal government worked in New York City. From 1790 to 1800, the Federal government worked in Philadelphia. The first session of the Supreme Court began with a four hour worship service. (Julia Duin, The Washington Times November 30, 2001, Friday, Pg. A2) Jay wanted the foundation of the new nation to be set correctly. In those days, the chief justices had to travel to the different circuits of the courts and Jay had to cover New England by stagecoach and stay in inns with fleas.

Washington sent Jay to England to negotiate a peace concerning British ships impressing (physically taking them off their own ship and making them work on British ships) American sailors. After all the debt of the American Revolution, we were in no financial shape to take on another war. Jay negotiated a treaty, known as the Jay Treaty with the British. Many Francophiles thought Jay gave too many concessions to the British and hung Jay in effigy. When Jay came back to the United States, he found out he had been elected governor of New York.

Jay retired from public service in 1802 and, sadly, his dear wife Sally died that same year. He worked with local Bible societies and missions groups. In 1822 he became the President of the American Bible Society. He was getting on in years and he could not travel much. His presidency consisted in being a figure head but it was a presidency nonetheless. He did not say "A Supreme Court justice should have nothing to do with God or the Bible." Being the president of a Bible society was a normal outflow of his life. He maintained the habit of morning and evening prayers even when guests came to visit.

As governor of New York, Jay outlawed slavery. He corresponded with William Wilberforce, who was instrumental in getting rid of slavery in the British Empire. John's son, William Jay, carried on with the abolitionist movement.

One of the most neglected pieces of literature about the American Revolution is Jay's address on December 23, 1776. The title is very boring but the content is powerful! "The Address of the Convention of the Representatives of the State of New York" is the name of the speech. William wrote a biography of his father in 1833, four years after John's death. Here is what William said of the speech: 'In this moment of gloom and dismay, Mr. Jay called on his countrymen, in language, perhaps the most thrilling that ever flowed from his pen, to awaken to a sense of danger, and to discharge the duties they owed to themselves, their country, and their God."

The Address of the Convention of the Representatives of the State of New York to Their Constituents

"At this most important period, when the freedom and happiness, or the slavery and misery, of the present and future generations of Americans is to be determined on a **solemn appeal to the Supreme Ruler of all events**, to whom every individual must one day answer for the part he now acts, it becomes the duty of the Representatives of a free people to call their attention to this most serious subject, and the more so at a time when their enemies are industriously endeavoring to delude, intimidate, and seduce them by false suggestions, artful misrepresentations, and insidious promises of protection.

"You and all men **were created free**, and authorized to establish civil government, for the preservation of your rights against oppression, and the security of that freedom **which God hath given you**, against the rapacious hand of tyranny and lawless power. It is, therefore, not only necessary to the well-being of Society, but the duty of every man, to oppose and repel all those, by whatever name or title distinguished, who prostitute the powers of Government to destroy the happiness and freedom over whom they may be appointed to rule.

"**Under the auspices and direction of Divine Providence**, your forefathers removed to the wilds and wilderness of America. By their industry they made it a fruitful, and by their virtue a happy country. And we should still enjoy the blessings of peace and plenty, if we had not forgotten **the source from which these blessings flowed**; and permitted our country to be contaminated by the many shameful vices which have prevailed among us.

"It is a well known truth, that no virtuous people were ever oppressed; and it is also true, that a scourge was never wanting to those of an opposite character. Even **the Jews, those favourites of Heaven**, met with the frowns, whenever they forgot the smiles of their **benevolent Creator**. By tyrants of Egypt, of Babylon, of Syria, and of Rome, they were severely chastised; and those tyrants themselves, when they had executed the vengeance of **Almighty God**, their own crimes bursting upon their own heads, received the rewards justly due to their violation of the sacred rights of mankind.

You were born equally free with the Jews, and have as good a right to be exempted from the arbitrary domination of Britain, as they had from the invasions of Egypt, Babylon, Syria, or Rome. But they, for their wickedness, were permitted to be scourged by the latter; and we, for our wickedness, are scourged by tyrants as cruel and implacable as those. Our case, however, is peculiarly distinguished from theirs. Their enemies were strangers, unenlightened, and bound to them by no ties of gratitude or consanguinity. **Our enemies, on the contrary, call themselves Christians**. They are of a nation and people bound to us by the strongest ties—a people, by whose side we have fought and bled; whose power we have contributed to raise; who owe much of their wealth to our industry, and whose grandeur has been augmented by our exertions.

It is unnecessary to remind you that during the space of between one and two hundred years, **every man sat under his own vine and his own fig-tree**, and there was none to make us afraid—that the people of Britain never claimed a right to dispose of us, and everything belonging to us, according to their will and pleasure, until the reign of the present King of that Island—and that to enforce this abominable claim they have invaded our country by sea and land. From this extravagant and iniquitous claim, and from the unreasonable as well as cruel manner in which they would gain our submission, it seems as though **Providence** were determined to use them as instruments to punish the guilt of this country, and bring us back to a sense of duty to **our Creator**.

You may remember that to obtain redress of the many grievances to which the King and Parliament of Great Britain had subjected you, the most dutiful petitions were presented, not only by the several Assemblies, but by the Representatives of all America in General Congress. And you cannot have forgot with what contempt they were neglected; nay, the humblest of all petitions, praying only to be heard, was answered by the sound of the trumpet and the clashing of arms. This, however, is not the only occasion on which the hearts of kings have been hardened; and in all probability it will add to the number of those instances in which their oppression, injustice and hardness of heart have worked their destruction.

Being bound by the strongest obligations to defend the inheritance which **God hath given us**, to **Him** we referred our Cause, and opposed the assaults of our taskmasters, being determined rather to die free than live slaves and entail bondage on our children.

By our vigorous efforts and by the goodness of **Divine Providence**, those cruel invaders were driven from our country in the last Campaign. We then flattered ourselves that the signal success of our arms, and the unanimity and spirit of our people, would have induced our foes to desist from the prosecution of their wicked designs, and disposed their hearts to peace. But peace we had not yet deserved. Exultation took place of thanksgiving, and we ascribed that to our own prowess which was only to be attributed to **the great Guardian of the innocent**.

The enemy with greater strength again invade us—invade us not less by their arts than their arms. They tell you that if you submit you shall have protection; that their king breathes nothing but peace; that he will revise (not repeal) all his cruel acts and instructions, and will receive you into favor. But what are the terms on which you are promised peace? Have you heard of any except absolute, unconditional obedience and servile submission? If his professions are honest—if he means not to cajole and deceive you, why are you not explicitly informed of the terms, and whether parliament means to tax you hereafter at their will and pleasure? Upon this and the like points, these military commissioners of peace are silent; and, indeed, are not authorized to say a word, unless a power to grant pardon implies a power to adjust claims and secure privileges; or unless the bare possession of life is the only privilege which Americans are to enjoy. For a power to grant pardon is the only one which their parliament or prince have thought proper to give them. And yet they speak of peace, but hold daggers in their hands, They invite you to accept of blessings, and stain your habitations with blood. **Their voice resembles the voice of Jacob, but their hands are like the hands of Esau.**

If their Sovereign intends to repeal any of the acts we complain of, why are they not especially named? If he designs you shall be free, why does he not promise that the claim of his parliament, to bind you in all cases whatsoever, shall be given up and relinquished? If a reasonable peace was intended, why did he not empower his Commissioners to treat with the Congress, or with Deputies from all the Assemblies; or why was not some other mode devised, in which America might be heard? Is it not highly ridiculous for them to pretend that they are authorized to treat of a peace between Britain and America with every man they meet? Was such a treaty ever heard of before? Is such an instance to be met with in the history of mankind? No! The truth is, peace is not meant; and their specious pretentions and proclamations are calculated only to disunite and deceive.

If the British king really desires peace, why did he order all your vessels to be seized, and confiscated? Why did he most cruelly command, that the men found on board such vessels should be added to the crews of his ships of war, and compelled to fight against their own countrymen—to spill the blood of their neighbors and friends; nay, of their fathers, their brothers and their children; and all this before these pretended ambassadors of peace had arrived on our shores! Does any history, sacred or profane, record any thing more horrid, more impious, more execrably wicked, tyrannical or devilish? If there be one single idea of peace in his mind, why does he order your cities to be burned, your country to be desolated, your brethren to starve, and languish, and die in prison? If any thing were intended besides destruction, devastation, and bloodshed, why are the mercenaries of Germany transported near four thousand miles to plunder your houses; ravish your wives and daughters; strip your infant children; expose whole families naked, miserable, and forlorn, to want, to hunger, to inclement skies, and wretched deaths? If peace were not totally reprobated by him, why are those pusillanimous, deluded, servile wretches among you, who, for present ease or impious bribes, would sell their liberty, their children, and their souls; who, like savages, worship every devil that promises not to hurt them; or obey any mandates, however cruel, for which they are paid? how is it, that these sordid, degenerate creatures, who bow the knee to this king, and daily offer incense at his shrine; should be denied the peace so repeatedly promised them? Why are they indiscriminately abused, robbed, and plundered, with their more deserving neighbors? **But in this world, as in the other, it is right and just that the wicked should be punished by their seducers.**

In a word, if peace was the desire of your enemies, and humanity their object, why do they thus trample under foot every right and every duty, human and divine? Why, like the demons of old, is their wrath to be expiated only by human sacrifices? Why do they excite the savages of the wilderness to murder our inhabitants and exercise cruelties unheard of among civilized nations? No regard for religion or virtue remains among them. Your very churches bear witness of their impiety; your churches are used without hesitation as jails, as stables, and as houses of sport and theatrical exhibitions. What faith, what trust, what confidence, can you repose in these men, who are deaf to the call of humanity, dead to every sentiment of religion, and void of all regard for the **temples of the Lord of Hosts?**

And why all this desolation, bloodshed, and unparalleled cruelty? They tell you to reduce your obedience. Obedience to what? To their will and pleasure! And then what? Why, then you shall be pardoned, because you consent to be slaves. And why should you be slaves now, having been freemen ever since this country was settled? Because, forsooth, the king and parliament of an island three thousand miles off, choose that you should be hewers of wood and drawers of water for them. And is this the people whose proud domination you are taught to solicit? Is this the peace which some of you so ardently desire? For shame! for shame!

But you are told that their armies are numerous, their fleet strong, their soldiers valiant, their resources great; that you will be conquered; that victory ever attends their standard; and therefore that your opposition is vain, your resistance fruitless. What then? You can but be slaves at last, if you should think life worth holding on so base a tenure. But who is it that gives victory? By whom is a nation exalted? Since what period hath the race been always to the swift and the battle to the strong? Can you be persuaded that the merciful **King of kings** hath surrendered His crown and sceptre to the merciless tyrant of Britain and committed the affairs of this lower world to his guidance, control and direction? We learned otherwise from our fathers; and **God himself** hath told us that strength and numbers avail not against Him. Seek then to be at peace with Him; solicit His alliance, and fear not the boasted strength and power of your foes.

You may be told that your forts have been taken, your country ravaged, and that your armies have retreated, and therefore that **God** is not with you. It is true that some forts have been taken, that our country hath been ravaged, and that **our Maker** is displeased with us. But it is also true that **the King of Heaven** is not like the King of Britain, implacable. If **His** assistance be sincerely implored, it will surely be obtained. If we turn from our sins, **He** will turn from **His** anger. Then will our arms be crowned with success, and the pride and power of our enemies, like the arrogance and **pride of Nebuchadnezzar**, will vanish away. Let us do our duty and victory will be our reward. Let a general reformation of manners take place; let no more widows and orphans, compelled to fly from their peaceful abodes, complain that you make a market of their distress, and take cruel advantage of their necessities; when your country is invaded and cries aloud for your aid, fly not to some secure corner of a neighboring State and remain idle spectators of her distress, but share in her fate and manfully support her cause; let universal charity, public spirit and private virtue be inculcated, encouraged and practised; unite in preparing for a vigorous defence of your country, as if all depended on your own exertions; and when you have done these things, then rely upon the **good Providence of Almighty God** for success, in full confidence, that without **His blessing** all our efforts will evidently fail.

A people moving on these solid principles never have been, and never will be, subjected by any tyrant whatever. **Cease, then, to desire the flesh-pots of Egypt, and remember their taskmasters and oppressions**. No longer hesitate about rejecting all dependence on a king who will rule you only with a rod of iron. Tell those who blame you for declaring yourselves independent that you have done no more than what your late king had done for you; that he declared you to be out of his protection; that he absolved you from all allegiance; that he made war upon you, and instead of your king he became your enemy and destroyer. By his consent, by his own act, you became independent of his crown. If you are wise you will always continue so. Freedom is now in your power. Value **the heavenly gift**. Remember, if you dare to neglect or despise it, you offer an insult to **the Divine Bestower**. Nor despair of keeping it. Despair and despondency mark a little mind and indicate a grovelling spirit. After the armies of Rome had been repeatedly defeated by Hannibal, that Imperial City was besieged by this brave and experienced general at the head of a numerous and victorious army. But so far were her glorious citizens from being dismayed by the loss of so many battles and of all their country, so confident in their own virtues and the protection of Heaven, that the very land on which the Carthaginians were encamped was sold at public auction for more than the usual price. Those heroic citizens disdained to receive his protection or to regard his proclamations. They remembered that their ancestors had left them free—ancestors who had bled in rescuing their country from the tyranny of kings. They invoked the protection **of the Supreme Being**. They bravely defended their city with undaunted resolution; they repelled the enemy and recovered their country. Blush, then, ye degenerate spirits; who give all over for lost, because your enemies have marched over three or four counties in this and a neighboring State—ye who basely fly to have the yoke of slavery fixed upon your necks and to swear that you and your children after you shall be slaves forever! Such men deserve to be slaves, and are fit only for beasts of burden to the rest of mankind. Happy would it be for America if they were removed away, instead of continuing in this Country to people it with a race of animals who, from their form, must be classed among human species, but possess none of those qualities which render man more respectable than the brutes.

There never yet was a war in which victory and success did not sometimes change sides. In the present, nothing has happened either singular or decisive. Inquire dispassionately, and be not deceived by those artful tales which emissaries so industriously circulate.

A powerful and well-disciplined army, supported by a respectable fleet, invade this country. They are opposed by an army which, though numerous and brave, is quite undisciplined. Notwithstanding this manifest disparity, they have never thought it prudent to give us battle, though they have often had the fairest opportunities. True it is, that taking advantage of that critical moment when our forces are almost disbanded, they have penetrated into Jersey, and marched a considerable distance without being attacked. If any are alarmed at this circumstance, let them consider that we do not fight for a few acres of land, but for freedom—for the freedom and happiness of millions yet unborn.

Would it not be highly imprudent to risk such important events upon the issue of a general battle, when it is certain Great Britain cannot long continue the war, and by protracting it we cannot fail of success? The British Ministry, sensible of this truth, and convinced that the people of England are aware of it, have promised that the present campaign shall be the last. They are greatly and justly alarmed at their situation. A country drained of men and money, the difficulties of supplying fleets and armies at so great a distance, the danger of domestic insurrections, the probability that France will take advantage of their defenseless condition, the ruin of their commerce by our privateers—these are circumstances at which the boldest are dismayed. They are convinced that the people will not remain long content in such a dangerous situation: hence it is that they press so hard to make this campaign decisive; and hence it is that we should endeavor to avoid it. Even suppose that Philadelphia, which many believed to be of such great importance, suppose it was taken or abandoned, the conquest of America will still be at a great distance. Millions, determined to be free, still remain to be subdued—millions who disdain to part with their liberties, their consciences, and the happiness of their posterity in future ages, for infamous protections and dishonorable pardons...

Whoever, therefore, considers the natural strength and advantage of this country, the distance it is removed from Britain, the obvious policy of many European Powers, the great supplies of arms and ammunition cheerfully afforded us by the French and Spaniards, and the feeble and destitute condition of Britain—that she is drained of men and of money, obliged to hire foreign mercenaries for the execution of her wicked purposes; in arrears to her troops for a twelve month's pay, which she cannot or will not discharge: her credit sunk; her trade ruined; her inhabitants divided; her King unpopular, and her Ministers execrated; that she is overwhelmed with a monstrous debt; cut off from the vast revenue heretofore obtained by taxes on American produce; her West India Islands in a starving condition; her ships taken; her merchants involved in bankruptcy; her design against us wicked, unjust, cruel, contrary **to the laws of God** and man, pursued with implacable, unrelenting vengeance, and in a manner barbarous and opposed to the usage of civilized nations;—whoever considers that we have humbly sought peace and been refused; that we have been denied even a hearing; all our petitions rejected; all our remonstrances disregarded; that we fight not for conquest but only for security; that our cause is the cause of **God**, of human nature and posterity: whoever we say seriously considers these things, must entertain very improper ideas of **the Divine justice** to which we have appealed, and be very little acquainted with the course of human affairs, to harbor the smallest doubt of our being successful...

This practice is not only consistent with human reason, but perfectly consonant to the will and practice of **God himself**. You know that the Jews were under **his peculiar direction**, and you need not be informed of the many instances in which **he** took the crown from such of their kings as refused to govern according to the laws of the Jews.

If then, **God hath given us freedom**, **are we responsible to him** for that, as well as other talents? If it be our birthright, let us not sell it for a mess of pottage, nor suffer it to be torn from us by the hand of violence! If the means of defence are in our power and we do not make use of them, what excuse shall we make to our children and **our Creator**? These are questions of the deepest concern to us all. These are questions which materially affect our happiness, not only in this world but in the world to come. And surely, "if ever a test for the trial of spirits can be necessary, it is now. If ever those of liberty and faction ought to be distinguished from each other, it is now. If ever it is incumbent on the people to know truth and to follow it, it is now." Rouse, therefore, brave Citizens! Do your duty like men! and be persuaded that **Divine Providence** will not permit this Western World to be involved in the horrors of slavery. Consider that, from the earliest ages of the world, Religion, Liberty and Empire, have been bounding their course toward the setting sun. The Holy Gospels are yet to be preached to those western regions, and we have the highest reason to believe that **the Almighty** will not suffer Slavery and the Gospel to go hand in hand! It cannot, it will not be.

But if there be any among us, dead to all sense of honor, and love of their country; if deaf to all the calls of liberty, virtue, and religion; if forgetful of the magnanimity of their ancestors, and the happiness of their children; if neither the examples nor the success of other nations, the dictates of reason and of nature, or the great duties they owe to their <u>God</u>, themselves, and their posterity, have any effect upon them; if neither the injuries they have received, the prize they are contending for, the future blessings or curses of their children, the applause or the reproach of all mankind, the approbation or displeasure of **the Great Judge**, or the happiness or misery consequent upon their conduct, in this and a future state, can move them;—then let them be assured, that they deserve to be slaves, and are entitled to nothing but anguish and tribulation. Let them banish from their remembrance the reputation, the freedom, and the happiness they have inherited from their forefathers. Let them forget every duty, human and divine; remember not that they have children: and beware how they call to mind the justice of **the Supreme Being**: let them go into captivity, like the idolatrous and disobedient Jews, and be a reproach and a by-word among the nations.

But we think better things of you. We believe, and are persuaded, that you will do your duty like men, and cheerfully refer your cause to the great and righteous Judge. If success crown your efforts, all the blessings of Freedom will be your reward. If you fail in the contest, you will be happy **with God and Liberty in Heaven**.

By the unanimous order of the Convention:

AB'M TEN BROECK, President
FISHKILL, December 23rd 1776

The address is very lengthy and this present copy has been edited by the writer to cut down on further length. However, this is one of the best defenses of the American Revolution from a biblical point of view. According to my calculations, there are 33 references to God, 6 more using the pronoun He, Him or His, and other biblical citations such as Nebuchadnezzar, Egypt, Babylon, Esau, etc. Jay cites the appeal to Heaven which Washington and others used. Jay noted that the Americans did not simply go to war, they tried everything in their power to stop it. Please remember that Jay was one who was holding out for peace and was against the war up until the writing of the Declaration of Independence. Once that was written, there was no turning back.

Jay was wrong about some things. He stated that God would not allow slavery and the Gospel would not be allowed to go hand in hand. This shows where Jay's heart was. As stated in <u>Can a Chief Justice Love God?: The Life of John Jay</u>, Jay was involved in the anti-slavery movement. He corresponded with William Wilberforce and became good friends with him while in England. John outlawed slavery in New York when he became the second governor. John's son William carried on the abolition of slavery struggle after his father died. Jay bought some slaves. He said that he would give them their freedom after a term of service. This may be seen in terms of indentured servants. John Adams had a clearer position- he did not have any slaves and did not want to get into the business in any fashion.

Elias Boudinot III

Benjamin Franklin knew Elias ever since he was a little boy. Franklin knew Elias' mother and father. When in Paris trying to get the Treaty of Paris (1783) worked out, Franklin talked at length about Elias being baptized by George Whitefield when he was young. When Elias was near his seventeenth birthday, he wanted to study for the ministry. However, family finances would not allow it.

Elias' grandfather was from Marans, which is 11 miles from La Rochelle (the Huguenot stronghold). Elias I left France in 1685 and became a British citizen and then moved to New York in 1687. Elias II moved to New Jersey where he had bought some land. Elias II was headed for the ministry but his father died and he had to support the family. He worked for seven years as a silversmith to Simeon Soumaine. The first wife of Elias II died in the early 1730s. His second marriage was to Catherine Williams. Not only was Elias III baptized by George Whitefield, but the pastor of his church was Gilbert Tennant.

Having Benjamin Franklin as a neighbor, many new conveniences came to the Boudinot family. The Franklin stove made rooms twice as warm and used one quarter the amount of wood formerly used. In the winter of 1746-47 there was some electricity. Fast forward to 1783- the little boy who was Franklin's neighbor in the 1740s was now the President of the Continental Congress (meeting in Annapolis, Maryland).

Elias II moved the family to Princeton in 1753. Elias had rented a house from the Rev. Burr in Princeton and was postmaster of Princeton.

Rev. Aaron Burr was the President of Princeton College when it opened in 1756. Burr's motto was from Psalm 119:64 "The earth, O Lord, is full of thy mercy, teach me thy statutes." Rev. Burr died in 1757 and left behind a one-year old orphan, Aaron Burr. Burr's father-in-law, Jonathan Edwards filled in as president from January to March and then died of smallpox.

In 1760, Elias III earned his law license and opened an office in Elizabethtown. He had hoped to be a minister, but since he could not afford college, he took up law. He met and married Hannah Stockton in 1762. He became president of the Board of Trustees of Princeton in 1765.

Alexander Hamilton arrived in 1772 with a letter from Hugh Knox to Elias Boudinot. Boudinot is interesting to read because one sees in his life the relationships between so many key leaders of the American Revolution. In the article about Hamilton, Hugh Knox was a graduate of Princeton.

In 1774 he went to the Continental Congress and was sent on a journey to Canada. William Livingston left the Continental Congress in June 1776. Livingston chose Boudinot as his aide-de camp. In January 1777, he was granted a commission as colonel and Commissary General of Prisoners. At one time in 1777 there were as many as 2,000 prisoners at the barracks at Lancaster, Pennsylvania. Boudinot tried to talk with the British about their treatment of American prisoners. Provost Marshall Cunningham sold the food and fuel meant for American prisoners and left the prisoners to starve and forage for food. Cunningham thought nothing of beating prisoners to death if they did not respond quickly enough to his orders. Here is Elias' letter to Hannah on Jan. 4, 1778:

> "...when I was called to my present Employment, not from any desire of increasing either my Wealth or Importance, but from an abhorrence of being an idle Spectator in of my Country's Distress, and a passionate Fondness for obliging our worthy General. I acknowledge that my devoutest and most constant Prayers at the Throne of Grace have been, that God would direct, lead and appoint me to such usefulness in Life as would most glorify his holy name, for if his will is done with and by me, I care not what department or what difficulties of Life I am called to. I have indeed kept a watchful Eye on all his Providences toward me, and can safely say, that they have been altogether kind & gracious."

Boudinot was on the verge of bankruptcy. When there was a prisoner exchange he put $26,666.66 on his credit so that he could suit the 300 officers and 1100 soldiers.

In 1778 he was elected to represent New Jersey in the Continental Congress. Congress held some sessions in College Hall, which was once the church where he grew up.

Rev. Caldwell was the pastor of the church which William Livingston and Elias Boudinot and others attended. In June, 1780 the British attacked Elizabethtown. A Tory shot through the window and killed Mrs. Caldwell. Rev. Caldwell heard about it later while he was chaplain for the troops and helped soldiers find packing for their muskets by offering pages from hymnals. The phrase "Give 'em Watts, boys!" came from that incident. Later that year, Rev. Caldwell died and left 9 orphans behind. John Edwards Caldwell was adopted by Lafayette and later helped Boudinot found the American Bible Society. Elias Boudinot Caldwell was adopted by Elias Boudinot. How could he not adopt a boy who was named after him?

On November 4, 1782 he was elected President of the Continental Congress. While president, he said the following: "God has ever been the director of our Paths and the Guide of our Ways. It is not the first Time that he has led us in the way which we know not- and set our Feet in a Strong Place. We have embarked in his Service, and it is our part to see that we do his will and act with a single Eye to his Glory and all will be well."

George Washington wrote to Boudinot about the same subject on April 12, 1783: "Thus far we may truly say, that we have passed thro' the wilderness by a series of Miracles, which nothing short of the over-ruling Providence of God could ever have wrought."

Boudinot and others were influential in Ohio becoming a state. He was given the job of overseeing the Federal Mint. When he retired from public office, he worked with others to found the American Bible Society. He served as its first President.

John Caldwell, son of Rev. Caldwell became a Catholic. The preconceived ideas of bigotry of some would dictate that Boudinot would reject John Caldwell from that point on. Au contrare, mon ami! John Caldwell was on the board of the American Bible Society.

"Do not suppose that I am so void of Christian Charity or ignorant of the Principles and Practices of thousands of the Roman Church, as to suppose that a Man may not, under the influence of them, lead a life of holiness & devotion to God- indeed may not arrive to the highest grade of the Christian Character. No, I am satisfied that the Grace of God is not confined to Sect or Party." May 2, 1790

Thomas Paine, Common Sense and The Age of Reason

The objective reader of <u>Common Sense</u> and <u>The Age of Reason</u> will find two different Thomas Paines. The atheistic/deistic camp has used Paine heavily since the 1960s. One will find the atheist strand in <u>The Age of Reason</u>. Many writers make a direct link between Thomas Paine and the other Founders by saying that Paine's writings "prove" that the Founders were deists and atheists. That argument can be countered with two points: 1) an objective reading of Common Sense and 2) what the Founders said about Paine during the <u>Common Sense</u> period contrasted with <u>The Age of Reason</u> period.

Common Sense hit a vein with the American public. It sold over 100,000 copies. That is a high figure for a population of about 3 million at the time of the American Revolution. With our current population of 300,000,000 the book would sell 10,000,000 copies today. Why did it sell so many copies? Was it because it was atheistic or was it because it had a basic Christian world?

Paine studied in a grammar school until he was thirteen and then became an apprentice to his father as a corset maker. His father was a Quaker. At age twenty he left his home to be a sailor aboard the ship King of Prussia in Britain's war with France. In the seaside town of Sandwich, he started a business that failed. In 1761 he was an exciseman in the district of Lincolnshire. He later lost that job and was destitute in London when he met Ben Franklin. Franklin encouraged him to seek a new life in the Colonies. Paine's first wife had died and he was separated from his second wife when he left England. He landed in Philadelphia and got a job in a printery. The print shop where he worked was only four blocks from Independence Hall. He fell into the center of activity.

Read Common Sense with common sense to see if there was a Christian worldview. When reading Common Sense for the first time, does anything jump out at you? What did Paine put in all capital letters for emphasis?

THE LORD SHALL REIGN OVER YOU
The Lord said unto Samuel, Hearken unto the voice of the people in all that they say unto thee, for they have not rejected thee, but they have rejected me,
THAT I SHOULD NOT REIGN OVER THEM

WE HAVE ADDED UNTO OUR SINS, THIS EVIL, TO ASK A KING.

One of the sayings of the American Revolution was "NO KING BUT KING JESUS"

Either Paine is hitting on a common theme here or is leading the way. A lot of sermons of the day seem to show it was a common theme. For more on this read <u>Political Sermons of the American Founding Era 1730-1805</u> edited by Ellis Sandoz.

Returning to Common Sense, Paine says the following about monarchy: "Tis a form of government which the word of God bears testimony against, and blood will attend it." (p. 18) "Even the distance at which the Almighty hath placed England and America, is a strong and natural proof, that the authority of the one ove the other, was never the design of Heaven." (p. 23) "Every quiet method for peace hath been ineffectual. Our prayers have been rejected with disdain." (p. 25)

"But where, says some, is the King of America? I'll tell you Friend, he reigns above and doth not make havoc of mankind like the Royal Brute of Britain. Yet that we may not appear to be defective even in earthly honors, let a day be solemnly set apart for proclaiming the charter, let it be brought forth placed on the divine law, the word of God; let a crown be placed thereon, by which the world may know, that so far as we approve of monarchy, that in America, THE LAW IS KING." (p.31)

"As to religion, I hold it to be the indispensable duty of all government, to protect all conscientious professors thereof, and I know of no other business which government hath to do therewith...For myself, I fully and conscientiously believe, that it is the will of the Almighty, that there should be diversity of religious opinions among us: It affords a larger field for our Christian kindness. Were we all of one way of thinking, our religious dispositions would want matter for probation; and on this liberal principle, I look on the various denominations among us, to be like children of the same family, differing only, in what is called, their Christian names." (p.39)

"We have it in our power to begin the world over again. A situation, similar to the present, hath not happened since the days of Noah until now." (p.48)

In his address to the Quakers at the end of Common Sense, Paine addresses their pacifism in the time of distress. "The love and desire of peace is not confined to Quakerism, it is the natural as well as the religious wish of all denominations of men..."

Paine has a lot of saucy nerve when he corrects the Quakers: "Had ye the honest soul of Barclay ye would preach repentance to your king. Ye would tell the Royal Wretch his sins and warn him of eternal ruin... we do not complain against you because ye are Quakers but because ye pretend to be and are NOT Quakers."

"Tyranny, like hell, is not easily conquered." Are those the words of some rabid Fundamentalist? No, those words come from Thomas Paine in <u>The American Crisis</u> (Dec. 19, 1776). That pamphlet eloquently starts out with: "These are the times that try men's souls." George Washington and others would read these writings to the Continental Army. Reading further, Paine says the following:

> "I have as little suspicion in me as any man living, but my secret opinion has ever been, and still is, that GOD almighty will not give up a people to military destruction, or leave them unsupportedly to perish, who had so earnestly and so repeatedly sought to avoid the calamities of war, by every decent method which wisdom could invent. Neither have I so much of the infidel in me, as to suppose, that He has relinquished the government of the world, and given us up to the

care of devils; and as I do not, I cannot see on what grounds the king of Britain can look up to heaven for help against us. A common murderer, a highwayman, or a housebreaker, has as good a pretence as he."

Looking back at the end of the American Revolution, Paine looked back on the part he played. "I shall always feel an honest pride at the part I have taken and acted, and a gratitude to Nature and Providence for putting it in my power to be of some use to mankind." (April 19, 1783)

Paine was definitely impacted by the Christian worldview during his time in the United States. In fairness to Paine, he gave the proceeds from the sale of Common Sense to support the war cause. After the war, he appealed to Congress for repayment of services but did not get much. One can see how the lack of recognition for his sacrifices embittered him, much like Benedict Arnold. There is a lesson in handling disappointment here. Arnold and Paine sacrificed deeply. Many others sacrificed a lot also but there is a place to carry that disappointment. God can truly help us with that burden if we put it in His hands. With the loss of a child or spouse, a job or a house, God can help you cope.

When the hand of God is strong upon a culture, Satan throws his attention in that area also. The things of God in one generation may be strong but even within one generation the table can be turned. Go back and see what happened to the generation that came after Joshua came into the Promised Land. They forgot God in one generation. "After that whole generation had been gathered to their fathers, another generation grew up, who knew neither the LORD nor what he had done for Israel." Judges 2:10

God had His hand on the United States (as this book documents) in its founding. However, Satan was ready with his poison. One aspect of that poison came from a person caught up in revolutions for revolution's sake. This man lived his life as a professional revolutionary. There is an aspect of Judas here. There is excitement and action in revolutions but that kind of life is not what God intends. It is easier to tear down a building (whether real or pretend) than it is to build one with loving care. Something in Thomas Paine made him want to always fight. It is significant to note that his first wife died and that he left his second wife before coming to America in 1774 (did he have other women in America and France?) While in America, Paine had been with the right crowd and had done some very good things but in the end turned on Jesus. He made his deliberated choice.

Some readers may be offended at the strong tone delivered to Paine. It is Paine who attacks Christ and the Church. At least fifteen times he refers to the "Christian mythologists". He calls Christianity ridiculous many times and refers to it as a fraud at least three times. He calls the Bible a fraud and the resurrection of Jesus a fraud. He is the one doing the attacking. Reading <u>The Age of Reason</u> makes me feel like I am in a secular university religion classroom.

"Nothing that is here said can apply, even with the most distant respect, to the real character of Jesus Christ. He was a virtuous and amiable man" says Paine. That is tantamount to saying I think all these ridiculous fraudulent myths about Jesus are garbage. I trash his religion but I still respect him. Paine hits on the head, the stomach, a shot to the solar plexus, the groin, the knees, the feet, etc. and then says "Let's be friends and play nicely, please respect me."

He does not take the apostle Thomas' example about doubting far enough. He leaves Thomas as a doubter. Thomas, when confronted by the living Jesus, bowed down and confessed: "My Lord and my God!" With pride, Christians from India will love to explain to you how "doubting Thomas" doubted no more and took the message of the risen Christ to the Kerala area of India.

What was the reaction of the Founding Fathers and the American public to Paine's <u>The Age of Reason</u>? Let's see what Ben Franklin thought of it. Remember, Franklin was the one who encouraged him to come to America. Franklin was the one who wrote a letter of recommendation that helped Paine find a job in Philadelphia. Paine sent Franklin a manuscript of a similar work in the late 1780s (keep in mind Franklin died in 1790). Here is what Franklin wrote to Paine:

"Dear Sir,

"I have read your manuscript with some attention. By the argument it contains against a particular Providence, though you allow a general Providence, you strike at the foundations of all religion. For without the belief of a Providence, that takes cognizance of, guards, and guides, and may favor particular persons, there is no motive to worship a Deity, to fear his displeasure, or to pray for his protection. I will not enter into any discussion of your principles, though you seem to desire it. At present I shall only give you my opinion, that though your reasonings are subtle and may prevail with some readers, you will not succeed so as to change the general sentiments of mankind on that subject, and the consequence of printing this piece will be, a great deal of odium drawn upon yourself, mischief to you, and no benefit to others. He that spits against the wind, spits in his own face.

"But, were you to succeed, do you imagine any good would be done by it? You yourself may find it easy to live a virtuous life, without the assistance afforded by religion; you having a clear perception of the advantages of virtue, and the disadvantages of vice, and possessing a strength of resolution sufficient to enable you to resist common temptations. But think how great a portion of mankind consists of weak and ignorant men and women, and of inexperienced, inconsiderate youth of both sexes, who have need of the motives of religion to restrain them from vice, to support their virtue, and retain them in the practice of it till it becomes habitual, which is the great point for its security. And perhaps you are indebted to her originally, that is to your religious education, for the habits of virtue upon which you now justly value yourself. You might easily display your excellent talents of reasoning upon a less hazardous subject, and thereby obtain a rank with our most distinguished authors. For among us it is not necessary, as among the Hottentots, that a youth, to be raised into the company of men, should prove his manhood by beating his mother.

I would advise you, therefore, not to attempt unchaining the tiger, but to burn this piece before it is seen by any other person; whereby you will save yourself a great deal of mortification by the enemies it may raise against you, and perhaps a good deal of regret and repentance. If men are so wicked with religion, what would they be if without it. I intend this letter itself as a proof of my friendship, and therefore add no profession to it; but subscribe simply yours,

B. Franklin"

David Barton in Original Intent (pp. 130-133) has shown responses from other Founders to Paine:

John Adams wrote the following in response to The Age of Reason: "The Christian religion is, above all the religions that ever prevailed or existed in ancient or modern times, the religion of wisdom, virtue, equity and humanity, let the Blackguard [scoundrel] Paine say what he will."

Samuel Adams wrote a rebuke to Paine on Nov. 30, 1802: "When I heard you had turned your mind to a defence of infidelity, I felt myself much astonished and more grieved that you had attempted a measure so injurious to the feelings and so repugnant to the true interest of a great part of the citizens of the United States."

Benjamin Rush wrote a letter to John Dickinson describing Paine's book "absurd and impious."

Charles Carroll from Maryland described Paine's book as "blasphemous writings against the Christian religion."

John Witherspoon stated that Paine was "ignorant of human nature as well as an enemy to the Christian faith."

John Quincy Adams stated: "Mr. Paine has departed altogether from the principles of the Revolution."

John Jay, the first Chief Justice responded to Paine's book in a letter to Rev. Uzal Ogden by saying this: "...I have long been of the opinion that the evidence of the truth of Christianity requires only to be carefully examined to produce conviction in candid minds. Religion, morality and a virtuous and enlightened clergy will always be impediments to the progress and success of certain systems and designs, and therefore will not cease to experience both direct and indirect hostilities from those who meditate or embark on them." In other words, Christians be ready for opposition. His family's Huguenot background taught him that.

Elias Boudinot, President of the Continental Congress when the Treaty of Paris was signed in 1783, was stirred up so much that he wrote a book in response. Boudinot's book was entitled <u>Age of Revelation</u>. The book is hard to find but check it out. Here is a summation of what he thinks about Paine's book:

> "When I first took up this treatise, I considered it as one of those vicious and absurd publications, filled with ignorant declamation and ridiculous representations of simple facts, the reading of which, with attention, would be an undue waste of time; but afterwards, finding it often the subject of conversation, in all ranks of society; and knowing the author to be generally plausible in his language, and very artful in turning the clearest truths into ridicule, I determined to read it, with an honest design of impartiality examining into its real merits.
>
> "I confess, that I was much mortified to find, the whole force of this vain man's genius and art, pointed at the youth of America, and her unlearned citizens, (for I have no doubt, but that it was originally intended for them) in hopes of raising a skeptical temper and disposition in their minds, well knowing that this was the best inlet to infidelity, and the most effectual way of serving its cause, thereby sapping the foundations of our holy religion in their minds.
>
> "To Christians, who are well instructed in the Gospel of the Son of God, such expedients rather add confirmation to their faith. They were forewarned near two thousand years ago, of these things, by their great Lord and Master; 'that when the time should come, they might remember, that he had told them of them.' They indeed rest in this strong confidence, 'that when the Lord Jesus shall be revealed from heaven, with his mighty angels in flaming fire, he will take

vengeance on them, who know not God, and who obey not the Gospel of our Lord Jesus Christ....

"I chose to confine myself to the leading and essential facts of the Gospel, which are contradicted, or attempted to be turned into ridicule, by this writer [Paine]. I have endeavored to detect his falsehoods and misrepresentations, and to show his extreme ignorance of the divine scriptures, which he makes the subject of his animadventures- not knowing that 'they are the power of God unto salvation, to every one that believeth.'

Robert Treat Paine shared the same last name, although he was not related. Keep in mind that Thomas Paine arrived in the "United States" in 1775. Robert Treat Paine had a son in 1773 and named him Thomas (probably after the Disciple Thomas or a family member). Robert Treat Paine did not know of Thomas Paine the Skeptic. Robert Treat Paine's son Thomas had his name changed to Robert Treat Paine because he did not want to be associated with Thomas Paine the Infidel.

Having seen how many of the Founding Fathers weighed in on the subject, what did the American people think? Well, when Paine returned to the United States, there were riots in the ports when people found out. One instance was in Baltimore in 1802. Paine lived the remainder of his life as an outcast in New York. When he died, he was buried in a farm field because there was no cemetery that would accept his remains. There is some debate about Paine repenting of his attitude. Check out the evidence for yourself. However, the verdict of the Founding Fathers and the American people show that they were not in agreement with Paine's Age of Reason.

Supposed Separation of Church and State

Want to make a million dollars? Find 10,000 people who will bet you $100 that the words "separation of church and state" are in the First Amendment. The average American has probably heard that phrase at least 300 times and has accepted it. Would you accept that bet if someone offered it? Save yourself $100 and go check out a copy of the First Amendment of the Constitution. Invest that $100 you would have lost in a savings bond for posterity- your child, your grandchildren or a scholarship. I really don't want you to gamble.

> "Congress shall make no law respecting an establishment of religion, or prohibiting the free exercise thereof; or abridging the freedom of speech, or of the press; or the right of the people peaceably to assemble, and to petition the Government for a redress of grievances."

The words separation of church and state first appeared in a 1802 letter from Thomas Jefferson to Danbury Baptists (Connecticut). For the many people who push the "secular only" Quick history quiz:

When was the Constitution written?   Answer: 1787
Where was Jefferson at that time?   Answer: France

"Congress shall make no establishment of religion ...nor prohibit the free exercise thereof." When was the last time you heard the phrase: "nor prohibit the free exercise thereof?" Was it on ABC, CBS, NBC or CNN?

Northwest Ordinance and "Separation"

There is a fifteen year gap between the writing of the First Amendment and the words "separation of church and state." In light of that time gap, I would like to focus on the Northwest Ordinance. <u>The First Amendment was written the same year as the Northwest Ordinance</u>. The same basic group wrote and agreed to both documents. I hope you are sitting down if you hold firmly to the "separation of church and state" litany. Article Four says: "<u>religion and morality shall forever be encouraged</u>." I will repeat that for emphasis: "religion and morality shall forever be encouraged." In the context of 1787 this is what the Founders meant by the First Amendment:

1. Congress was not supposed to prohibit the free exercise of religion and
2. religion and morality shall forever be encouraged.

Let us examine how the Northwest Ordinance specifically encouraged religion.

Northwest Ordinance Specifics

Article Four of the Northwest Ordinance stated that religion and morality shall forever be encouraged. Let us look at some specific instances. "General tolerant Christianity" is wording which Daniel Webster, the Senator, referred to. You will see this in action as you examine how the Congress in 1787 (the same year as the First Amendment) spent limited government funds to encourage Christianity in many forms.

1801- Society of United Brethren-Cherokee nation
1817- American Board of Commissioners for Foreign Missions
1820- Hamilton Baptist Missionary Society of N.Y. for the Oneida
1821- Missionary Society of N.Y. for the Seneca

The Society of Friends, Methodists, Society for the Propagation of the Gospel, Cumberland Missionary Board, Episcopalians, etc. were paid federal money to establish schools and teach the arts of civilization and the doctrine of Christianity. (Separation of Church and State: Fact or Fiction? By Robert Cord)

Freedom of Religion, not Freedom From Religion

It's freedom of religion, not freedom from religion. One little word can make a huge difference. The Founders stood for religious freedom. They would be shocked to find out that the First Amendment has been hijacked to mean that there is no place for God in public matters. Many of the Founders went to church 2-3 times on Sundays. Many of them grew up going to churches where the sermon itself lasted over one hour. Many of them went to colleges where morning and evening prayers were attended. Many were tutored by ministers, or were the sons of ministers or grandsons of ministers.

To the Founders, God was very public. What kind of flag did George Washington put on his supply ships? An Appeal to Heaven Why are chaplains allowed in Congress and the military today? They were there from the very beginning and it is too well documented to cover up. Why is there a Bible at the Inauguration of the President? George Washington set the precedent and had the Bible opened. What was the seal that Jefferson and Franklin wanted for our country? Jefferson and Franklin wanted a drawing of the children of Israel at the parting of the Red Sea which said: "Rebellion to tyrants is obedience to God." To those who always hide behind Franklin and Jefferson, I know that is hard to take. Those heroes of the Deist argument side wanted to be publicly obedient to God.

What About Jefferson?

For many, Jefferson is the only spokesman for the Founders. It appears that only he has the definitive word about what viewpoint the Founders had concerning church and state relations. Jefferson was an extremely important man in the beginnings of our nation; however, there were other opinions which seem to be lost on our current observers. There was a Congress and he was not the only person in it. There were other presidents. There were 56 signers of the Declaration of Independence, he was one of them (although an important one). In looking at Jefferson's worldview, let us examine not just what is politically expedient in our present cultural setting. Let us see more of a breadth of his writings- Let us look afresh at his writings and his life. Of the Founding Fathers, Jefferson probably had one of the weakest Christian worldviews, if it should be classified as a Christian worldview at all. However, keep in mind, that as a reader in our current society you have probably read scores of accounts in magazines, newspapers and books attributing atheism or deism to Jefferson. What do his writings say? This portion on Jefferson will try to examine Jefferson's worldview.

Jefferson's father died when he was a young man. He had a happy marriage with Martha Skelton. When she died, he was devastated. His wife's death, coupled with his contact with French atheism crippled his Christian worldview. Of all of the signers of the Declaration of Independence, his worldview is one of the weakest. However, when he penned the Declaration, and his wife was living, it seemed to be stronger.

Jefferson was born in 1743 into the Central Piedmont area. The Great Awakening hit his area of Ablemarle County. A recommended book for deeper study on the topic is <u>Religion and Political Culture in Jefferson's Virginia</u> (edited by Garrett Ward Sheldon and Daniel L. Dreisbach). Another good reference is the Providence Foundation which is based in Charlottesville, Virginia.

An interesting point about the Great Awakening in that area was that interdenominational co-operation was common. Samuel Davies, John Todd, Devereaux Jarrett and John Waller had successful preaching campaigns in the area. Open-air meetings started during the 1770s (one had 5,000 in attendance). In 1776 between 71 and 77 percent of Americans may have filled the pews on Sunday... It is more accurate to characterize the years from 1775 to 1790 as a Revolutionary revival. [James H. Hutson, Religion and the Founding of the American Republic, pp 32-33]

Jefferson was tutored by evangelical Scottish clergyman William Douglas. His pastor was Charles Clay (an evangelical) when he became vestryman at St. Anne's Parish. Jefferson, along with Philip Mazzei and John Harvie organized a new independent church called the Calvinistic Reformed Church to demonstrate **his disestablishment conviction that institutional religion and clerical salaries should be wholly financed by voluntary contributions**. The church worshipped in the Ablemarle Courthouse in Charlottesville from 1777 to 1785. The church disbanded when its three large supporters moved away. Between 1801 and 1806, Ablemarle County was the hotbed of revivalism.

Concerning Charles Clay, Jefferson wrote the following on August 15, 1779:

> "In the earliest stage of the present contest with Great Britain, while the clergy of the established church in general took the adverse side, or kept aloof from the cause of the country, he took a decided and active part with his countrymen, and has continued to prove his whiggism [see my Jay book, p.6] unequivocal and his attachment to the American cause to be sincere and zealous." Clay was asked by Jefferson to preach

at a Fast Day service on July 23, 1774 which was attended by a great multitude of people.

Daniel Dreisbach, in chapter seven of the book brings up some excellent points. Many current treatments of Jefferson's views on religion [please repeat the "separation of church and state" mantra] focus on the Bill of Religious Freedom. The same day that the bill was entered (sponsored by Madison and endorsed by Jefferson), there were four other bills brought forth by Madison that dealt with religion.

- Bill 82- Bill of Religious Freedom
- Bill 83- Bill for Saving the Property of the Church Heretofore by Law Established
- Bill 84- Bill for Punishing Disturbers of Religious Worship and Sabbath Breakers [10 shilling fine]
- Bill 85- Bill for Appointing Days of Public Fasting and Thanksgiving [ministers had to pay £50 for not performing divine service]
- Bill 86- Bill Annulling Marriages Prohibited by the Levitical Law and Appointing the Mode for Solemnizing Lawful Marriage.

Many "separation of church and state" dogmatists may be scandalized to know that their man Jefferson was for 1) saving the property of the established church [even though he fought for the disestablishment of the state church, he was for the Anglican/Episcopal church keeping its property], 2) punishing Sabbath-breakers, 3) days of public fasting and thanksgiving and 4) supporting Biblical marriage instead of common law arrangements.

<u>Jefferson has more concerns for "separation of church and state" dogmatists</u>.
- In May 24, 1774 he helped draft a resolution appointing a day of fasting, humiliation and prayer
- As governor of Virginia in 1779, he issued a proclamation decreeing a day of publick and solemn thanksgiving and prayer

to Almighty God. [This goes along with his ideal that **states had the right, not the federal government, to appoint days of prayer**]

-In 1802 Jefferson signed into federal law tax exemption for churches in Alexandria County

-In an 1803 Treaty with the Kaskasians, the Federal government gave Catholic missions $700 toward the support of a priest

-Jefferson signed three extensions giving federal money to the United Brethren for the spreading of the Christian faith.

-the University of Virginia would allow, while under Jefferson, different schools of religion to set up on campus

-as President of the United States, worshipped regularly in the Capital building

-Jefferson, along with Franklin, proposed the following seal of the United States:

"Rebellion to tyrants is obedience to God."

Take note of what the "least" religious of the Founders said concerning God:

"I tremble for our nation when I consider that God is just."

If you read that on a wall somewhere in Washington, D.C., it is not graffiti from some religious nut; those are the words of Thomas Jefferson. They are inscribed in stone on the Jefferson Memorial. They have not yet been erased as of the last check.

Having discussed the positive side of Jefferson on religious issues there are some major glaring problems on the negative side. As said earlier, the death of his father at age 14, his wife dying in 1782 (he was 39), having only 2 daughters live to maturity, and the atheistic climate of France took quite a bit out of his Christian worldview. He objected to total depravity and rejected atonement passages. In his harmony of the Gospels, he omitted the miraculous sections. He denied that Jesus was a divine being but still maintained that Jesus was the greatest man that ever lived. He held Jesus in esteem as the Greatest Teacher.

C.S. Lewis' answer on such a question would be that one cannot call Jesus the Greatest Teacher if he said that He was God but really was not. He would be a monster of a liar. Lewis called Jesus either Lord, Lunatic or Liar. The rest of the Signers would not put up with such foolishness.

It appears that Jefferson was influenced by Lord Bolingbroke's writings. Bolingbroke had a strong skepticism about the historical nature of biblical accounts. In Jefferson's New Testament, all the writings of St. Paul are omitted. John Adams wrote the following about Bolingbroke's writings: "His Religion is a pompous Folly: and his Abuse of the Christian Religion is as superficial as it is impious." [Diary and Autobiography of John Adams, 3:264]

Concerning personal moral issues, there are problems with Sally Hemmings and Mrs. Conway in France. Even though the Monticello Foundation official policy says that Thomas Jefferson is the father of children by Sally Hennings, the DNA lab results state that it is someone in the Jefferson family. A comparison of who is in the area at what time frame [concerning conception time] seems to fit Randolph Jefferson more.

The alleged affair in France is not a proven fact in my mind. It could possibly be the truth. A suggestion could be given to Mr. Jefferson: instead of going these supposed routes, why not remarry?

In summary, Jefferson is probably the signer with one of the lowest, if not the lowest Christian worldview of the signers. Keep in mind that he does not speak for all the signers. Keep in mind the letter that Benjamin Rush sent to John Adams during Adams' retirement. Rush reminded Adams when Jefferson [in late summer of 1776] rose in opposition to a fast day and in so doing appeared to put down Christianity.

"You rose and defended the motion, and in reply to Mr. Jefferson's objections to Christianity you said you were sorry to hear such sentiments from a gentleman whom you so highly respected and with whom you agreed upon so many subjects, and that it was the only instance you had ever known of a man of sound sense and real genius that was an enemy to Christianity." [quoted in David McCullough's John Adams, p.113.]

<u>That quote speaks volumes of the Christian men in the Congress of 1776.</u>

DAYS OF PRAYER

April 15, 1775

Whereas it has pleased the righteous Sovereign of the Universe, in just indignation against the sins of a People long blessed with inestimable Priviledges, civil and religious, to suffer the Plots of wicked Men on both Sides of the Atlantic, who for many Years have incessantly laboured to sap the Foundation of our public Liberties, so far to succeed; that we see the New-England Colonies reduced to the ungrateful Alternative of a tame Submission to a State of absolute Vasallage to the Will of a despotick Minister- or of preparing themselves speedily to defend, at the Hazard of Life, the unalienable Rights of themselves and Posterity, against the avowed Hostilities of their Parent State, who openly threatens to wrest them from their Hands by Fire and Sword.

In Circumstances dark as these, it becomes us, as Men and Christians, to reflect that, whilst every prudent Measure should be taken to ward off the impending Judgments, or prepare to act a proper Part under them when they come; at the same Time, all Confidence must be with-held from the Means we use; and reposed only on that God, who rules in the Armies of Heaven, and without whose Blessing the best human Counsels are but Foolishness- and all created Power Vanity;

It is the Happiness of his Church that, when the Powers of Earth and Hell combine against it, and those who should be Nursing Fathers become its Persecutors- then the Throne of Grace is of the easiest Access- and its Appeal thither is graciously invited by the

Father of Mercies, who has assured it, that when his Children ask Bread he will not give them a Stone:

> Therefore, in Compliance with the laudable Practice of the People of GOD in all Ages, with humble Regard to the Steps of Divine Providence towards this oppressed, threatened and endangered People, and especially in Obedience to the Command of Heaven, that binds us to call on him in the Day of Trouble,-
> Resolved, That it be, and hereby recommended to the good people of this Colony, of all Denominations, That THURSDAY, the Eleventh Day of May next be set apart as a Day of Public Humiliation, Fasting and Prayer: that a total abstinence from servile Labor and Recreation be observed, and all their religious Assemblies solemnly convened, to humble themselves before GOD under the heavy Judgments felt and feared, to confess the Sins that have deserved them, to implore the Forgiveness of all our Transgressions, and a Spirit of Repentance and Reformation- and a Blessing on the Husbandry, Manufactures, and other lawful Employments of this People; and especially that the Union of the American Colonies in Defence of their Rights (for which hitherto we desire to thank Almighty GOD) may be preserved and confirmed- that the Provincial and especially the Continental CONGRESSES may be directed to such measures as GOD will countenance- That the People of Great Britain, and their Rulers, may have their Eyes open'd to discern the Things that shall make for the Peace of the Nation and all its Connexions- And that AMERICA may soon behold a gracious Interposition of Heaven, for the Redress of her many Grievances, the Restoration of all her invaded Liberties, and their Security to the latest Generations.

By the Order of the Provincial Congress,

JOHN HANCOCK, President

July 20, 1775

The committee, appointed for preparing a resolve for a fast, brought in a report, which, being read was agreed to as follows:

As the great Governor of the World, by his supreme and universal Providence, not only conducts the course of nature with unerring wisdom and rectitude, but frequently influences the minds of men to serve the wise and gracious purposes of his providential government; and it being, at all times, our indispensable duty devoutly to acknowledge his superintending providence, especially in times of impending danger and public calamity, to reverence and adore his immutable justice as well as to implore his merciful interposition for our deliverance:

This Congress, therefore, considering the present critical, alarming and calamitous state of these colonies, do earnestly recommend that Thursday, the 20th day of July next, be observed, by the inhabitants of all the English colonies on this continent, as a day of public humiliation, fasting and prayer; that we may, with united hearts and voices, unfeignedly confess and deplore our many sins; and offer up our joint supplications to the all-wise, omnipotent, and merciful Disposer of all events; humbly beseeching him to forgive our iniquities, to remove our present calamities, to avert those desolating judgments, with which we are threatened, and to bless our rightful sovereign, King George the third, and [to] inspire him with wisdom to discern and pursue the true interest of all his subjects, that a speedy end may be put to the civil discord between Great Britain and the American colonies, without further effusion of blood: And that the British nation may be influenced to regard the things that belong to her peace, before they are hid from her eyes: That these colonies may be ever under the care and protection of a kind Providence, and be prospered in all their interests; That the divine blessing may descend and rest upon all our civil rulers, and upon the representatives of the people, in their several assemblies and conventions, that they may be directed to wise and effectual measures for preserving the union, and securing the just rights and priviledges of the colonies; That virtue and true religion may revive and flourish throughout our land; And that all America may soon behold a gracious interposition of Heaven, for the redress of her many grievances, the restoration of her invaded rights, a reconciliation with the parent state, on terms constitutional and honorable to both; And that her civil and religious priviledges may be secured to the latest posterity.

And it is recommended to Christians, of all denominations, to assemble for public worship, and to abstain from servile labour and recreations on said day.

May 17, 1776

Mr. William Livingston, pursuant to leave granted, brought in a resolution for appointing a fast, which ∥ being taken into consideration, & par; was agreed to as follows:

In times of impending calamity and distress; when the liberties of America are imminently endangered by the secret machinations and open assaults of an insidious and vindictive administration, it becomes the indispensable duty of these hitherto free and happy colonies, with true penitence of heart, and the most reverent devotion, publickly to acknowledge the over ruling providence of God; to confess and deplore our offences against him; and to supplicate his interposition for averting the threatened danger, and prospering our strenuous efforts in the cause of freedom, virtue and posterity.

The **Congress**, therefore, considering the warlike preparations of the British Ministry to subvert our invaluable rights and priviledges, and to reduce us by fire and sword, by the savages of the wilderness, and our own domestics, to the most abject and ignominious bondage: Desirious, at the same time, to have people of all ranks and degrees duly impressed with a solemn sense of God's superintending providence, and of their duty, devoutly to rely, in all their lawful enterprises, on his aid and direction, Do earnestly recommend, that Friday, the Seventeenth day of May next, be observed by the said colonies as a day of humiliation, fasting and prayer; that we may, with united hearts, confess and bewail our manifold sins and transgressions, and, through the merits and mediation of Jesus Christ, obtain his pardon and forgiveness; humbly imploring his assistance to frustrate the cruel purposes of our unnatural enemies; and by inclining their hearts to justice and benevolence, prevent the further effusion of blood. But if, continuing deaf to the voice of reason and humanity, and inflexibly bent, on desolation and war, they constrain us to repel their hostile invasions by open resistance, that it may please the Lord of Hosts, the God of Armies, to animate our officers and soldiers with invincible fortitude, to guard and protect them in the day of battle, and to crown the continental arms, by sea and land, with victory and success: Earnestly beseeching him to bless our civil rulers, and the representatives of the people, in their several assemblies and conventions; to preserve and strengthen their union, to inspire them with an ardent, disinterested love of their country; to give them wisdom and stability to their counsels; and direct them to the most efficacious measures for establishing the rights of America on the most honourable and permanent basis—that he would be graciously pleased to bless all his people in these colonies with health and plenty, and grant that a spirit of incorruptible patriotism, and of pure undefiled religion, may universally prevail; and this continent be speedily restored to the blessings of peace and liberty, and enabled to transmit them inviolate to the latest posterity. And it is recommended to Christians of all denominations, to assemble for public worship, and abstain from servile labour on the said day.

[Printed in the Pennsylvania Gazette, 20 March, 1776

December 18, 1777

A PROCLAMATION
For a General Thanksgiving,
Throughout the United-States of AMERICA
In *CONGRESS,* November 1, 1777

Forasmuch as it is the indispensable Duty of all Men, to adore the superintending Providence of Almighty GOD, to acknowledge with Gratitude their Obligation to Him for Benefits received, and to implore such further Blessings as they stand in Need of; and it having pleased Him, in his abundant Mercy, not only to continue to us the innumerable Bounties of his common Providence; but also to smile upon us, in the Prosecution of a just and necessary WAR, for the Defence and Establishment of our unalienable Rights and Liberties; particularly, in that he hath been pleased in so great a Measure to prosper the Means used for the Support of our Troops, and to crown our Arms with most signal Success:

It is therefore recommended to the Legislature or executive Powers of these several **UNITED STATES**, to set apart **T H U R S D A Y**, the eighteenth Day of December next, for solemn **THANKSGIVING** and **PRAISE**: That at one Time and with one Voice the good People may express the grateful Feelings of their Hearts, and consecrate themselves to the Service of their Divine Benefactor; and that together with their sincere Acknowledgements and Offerings they may join the penitent Confession of their manifold Sins whereby they had forfeited every Favour, and their humble and earnest Supplication that **GOD**, thro' the Merits of *Jesus Christ*, would mercifully forgive and blot them out of Remembrance, that it may please him graciously to afford his Blessing on the Government of these states respectively, and prosper the public Council of the whole; to inspire our Commanders by Land and Sea, and all under them, with that Wisdom & Fortitude which may render them fit Instruments, under the Providence of Almighty GOD, to secure for these United States, the greatest of all human Blessings, Independence and Peace; that it may please him to prosper the Trade and Manufactures of the People, and the Labour of the Husbandman, that our Land may yield its Increase; to take Schools and Seminaries of Education, so necessary for the cultivating the Principles of true Liberty, Virtue, and Piety, under his nurturing Hand; and to prosper the Means of Religion for the Promotion and Enlargement of that Kingdom which consisteth in Righteousness, Peace and Joy in the Holy Ghost.

And it is further recommended, that servile Labour and Recreation, altho' at other Times innocent, may be unbecoming the Purpose of this Appointment, be omitted on so solemn an Occasion.

Extracted from the Minutes,
Attest,
Cha. Thompson, Secretary

GOD Save the UNITED-STATES of AMERICA

May 3, 1779

PROCLAMATION.

WHEREAS, In just Punishment of our manifold Transgressions, it hath pleased the Supreme Disposer of all Events to visit these United States with a calamitous War, through which his Divine Providence hath hitherto in a wonderful Manner conducted us, so that we might acknowledge that the Race is not to the Swift, nor the Battle to the Strong; AND WHEREAS, notwithstanding the Chastisements received and Benefits bestowed, too few have been sufficiently awakened to a Sense of their Guilt, or warmed with Gratitude, or taught to amend their Lives and turn from their Sins, that so he might turn his Wrath: AND WHEREAS, from a Consciousness of what we have merited at his Hands, and an Apprehension that the Malevolence of our disappointed Enemies, like the Incredulity of Pharaoh, may be used as the Scourge of Omnipotence to vindicate his slighted Majesty, there is Reason to fear that he may permit much of our Land to become the Prey of the Spoiler, our Borders to be ravaged, and our Habitations destroyed:

RESOLVED,

THAT it be recommended to the several States to appoint the First *Thursday* in *May* next to be a Day of Fasting, Humiliation, and Prayer to Almighty God, that he will be pleased to avert those impending Calamities which we have but too well deserved: That he will grant us his Grace to repent of our Sins, and amend our Lives according to his Holy Word: That he will continue that wonderful Protection which hath led us through the paths of Danger and Distress: That he will be a Husband to the Widow, and a Father to the fatherless Children, who weep over the Barbarities of a Savage Enemy: That he will grant us Patience in Suffering, and Fortitude in Adversity: That he will inspire us with Humility, Moderation, and Gratitude in prosperous Circumstances: That he will give Wisdom to our Councils, Firmness to our Resolutions, and Victory to our Arms: That he will bless the Labours of the Husbandman, and pour forth Abundance, so that we may enjoy the Fruits of the Earth in due Season: That he will cause Union, Harmony and mutual Confidence to prevail throughout these States: That he will bestow on our great Ally all those Blessings which may enable him to be gloriously instrumental in protecting the Rights of Mankind, and promoting the Happiness of his Subjects: That he will bountifully continue his paternal Care to the Commander in Chief, and the Officers and Soldiers of the United States: That he will grant the Blessings of Peace to all contending Nations, Freedom to those who are in Bondage, and Comfort to the Afflicted: That he will diffuse Useful Knowledge, extend the Influence of True Religion, and give us that Peace of Mind which the World cannot give: That he will be our Shield in the Day of Battle, our Comforter in the Hour of Death, and our kind Parent and merciful Judge through Time and Eternity.

Done in CONGRESS, this *Twentieth Day of March, in the Year of our Lord One Thousand Seven Hundred and Seventy-Nine, and in the Third Year of our Independence.*

JOHN JAY, President.
Attest. CHARLES THOMSON, Secretary.

April 29, 1780

The committee, appointed to prepare a recommendation to the several states to set apart the last Wednesday in April next as a day of fasting, humiliation and prayer, brought in a draught, which was read and agreed to, as follows:

It having pleased the righteous Governor of the World, for the punishment of our manifold offences, to permit the sword of war still to harass our country, it becomes us to endeavour, by humbling ourselves before him, and turning from every evil way, to avert his anger and obtain his favour and blessing: it is therefore hereby recommended to the several states,

That Wednesday, the twenty sixth day of April next, be set apart and observed as a day of fasting, humiliation and prayer, that we may, with one heart and one voice, implore the sovereign Lord of Heaven and Earth to remember mercy in his judgment; to make us sincerely penitent for our transgressions; to prepare us for deliverance, and to remove the evils with which he hath been pleased to visit us; to banish vice and irreligion from among us, and establish virtue and piety by his divine grace to revive and spread the influence of patriotism, and eradicate, that love and pleasure and of gain which renders us forgetful of our country and our God; to bless all public councils throughout the United States, giving them wisdom, firmness and unanimity, and directing them to the best measures for the public good; to bless the magistrates and people of every rank, and animate and unite the hearts of all to promote the interests of their country; to bless the public defence, inspiring all commanders and soldiers with magnanimity and perseverance, and giving vigor and success to the military operations by sea and land; to bless the illustrious Sovereign and the nation in alliance with these states, and all who interest themselves in the support of our rights and liberties; to make that alliance of perpetual and extensive usefulness to those immediately concerned, and mankind in general; to grant fruitful seasons, and to bless our industry, trade and manufactures; to bless all schools and seminaries of learning, and every means of instruction and education; to cause wars to cease, to the ends of the earth and to establish peace among the nations.

And it is further recommended, that servile labour and recreations be forbidden on the said day.

December 7, 1780

Congress took into consideration the resolution reported for setting apart a day of thanksgiving and prayer, and agreed to the following draught:

Whereas it hath pleased Almighty God, the Father of all mercies, amidst the vicissitudes and calamities of war, to bestow blessings on the people of these states, which call for their devout and thankful acknowledgements, more especially in the late remarkable interposition of his watchful providence, in recusing the person of our Commander in Chief and the army from imminent dangers, at the moment when treason was ripened for execution; in prospering the labours of the husbandmen, and causing the earth to yield its increase in plentiful harvest; and above all, in continuing to us the enjoyment of the gospel of peace;

It is therefore recommended to the several states to set apart Thursday, the seventh day of December next, to be observed as a day of public thanksgiving and prayer; that all the people may assemble on that day to celebrate the praises of our Divine Benefactor; to confess our unworthiness of the least of his favours, and to offer our fervent supplications to the God of all grace; that it may please him to pardon our heinous transgressions and incline our hearts for the future to keep all his laws that it may please him still to afford us the blessing of health; to comfort and relieve our brethren who are any wise afflicted or distressed; to smile upon our husbandry and trade and establish the work of our hands; to direct our publick councils, and lead our forces, by land and sea, to victory; to take our illustrious ally under his special protection, and favor our joint councils and exertions for the establishment of speedy and permanent peace; to cherish all schools and seminaries of education, build up his churches in their most holy faith and to cause the knowledge of Christianity to spread over all the earth.

Done in Congress, the 19th day of October, 1780 and in the fifth year of the independence of the United States of America.

May 3, 1781

The report of the committee appointed to prepare a recommendation to these states, to set apart a day of humiliation and prayer was taken into consideration; and thereupon

The United States in Congress assembled, agreed to the following proclamation:

In times of calamity and impending danger when a vindictive enemy pursues with unrelenting fury a war of rapine and devastation to reduce us by fire and sword, by the savages of the wilderness and our own domestics to the most adject and ignominious bondage; it becomes the indespensible duty of the citizens of the United States with true penitence of heart publicly to acknowledge the over ruling Providence of God, to confess our offences against him, and to supplicate his gracious interposition for averting the threatened danger and preparing our efforts in the defence and preservation of our injured country.

At all times it is our duty to acknowledge the over-ruling providence of the great Governor of the universe, and devoutly to implore his divine favour and protection. But in the hour of calamity and impending danger, when by fire and sword, by the savages of the wilderness, and by our own domestics, a vindictive enemy pursues a war of rapine and devastation, with unrelenting fury, we are peculiarly excited, with true penitence of heart, to prostrate ourselves before our great Creator, and fervently to supplicate his gracious interposition for our deliverance.

The United States in Congress assembled, therefore do earnestly recommend, that Thursday the third of May next, may be observed as a day of humiliation, fasting and prayer, that we may, with united hearts, confess and bewail our manifold sins and transgressions, and by sincere repentance and amendment of life, appease his righteous displeasure, and through the merits of our blessed Saviour, obtain pardon and forgiveness: that it may please him to inspire our rulers with wisdom and uncorruptible integrity, and to direct and prosper their councils: to inspire all our citizens with a fervent and disinterested love of their country, and to preserve and strengthen their union:

to turn the hearts of the disaffected, or to frustrate their devices: to regard with divine compassion our friends in captivity, affliction and distress, to comfort and relieve them under their sufferings, and to change their mourning into grateful songs of triumph: that it may please him to bless our ally, and to render the connection formed between these United States and his kingdoms a mutual and lasting benefit to both nations: to animate our officers by sea and land with invincible fortitude, and to guard and protect them in the day of battle, and to crown our joint endeavours for terminating the calamities of war with victory and success: that the blessings of peace and liberty may be established on an honourable and permanent basis, and transmitted inviolate to the latest posterity: that it may please him to prosper our husbandry and commerce, and to bless us with health and plenty: that it may please him to bless all schools and seminaries of learning, and to grant that truth, justice and benevolence, and pure and undefiled religion, may universally prevail.

And it is recommended to all the people of these states, to assemble for public worship, and abstain from labour on the said day.

April 25, 1782

On a report of a committee, consisting of Mr. [Joseph] Montgomery, Mr. [Oliver] Wolcott, and Mr.[John Morin] Scott appointed to prepare a recommendation to the several states, to set apart a day of humiliation, fasting, and prayer Congress agreed to the following

Proclamation:

The goodness of the Supreme Being to all his rational creatures, demands their acknowledgements of gratitude and love; his absolute government of this world dictates, that it is the interest of every nation and people ardently to supplicate his mercy favor and implore his protection.

When the lust of dominion or lawless ambition excites arbitrary power to invade the rights, or endeavor to wrench wrest from a people their sacred and unalienable invaluable privileges, and compels them, in defence of the same, to encounter all the horrors and calamities of a bloody and vindictive war; then is that people loudly called upon to fly unto that God for protection, who hears the cries of the distressed, and will not turn a deaf ear to the supplication of the oppressed.

Great Britain, hitherto left to infatuated councils, and to pursue measures repugnant to their her own interest, and distressing to this country, still persists in the chimerical idea design of subjugating these United States; which will compel us into another active and perhaps bloody campaign.

The United States in Congress assembled, therefore, taking into consideration our present situation, our multiplied transgressions of the holy laws of God, and his past acts of kindness and goodness exercised towards us, which we would ought to record with the liveliest gratitude, think it their indispensable duty to call upon the different several states, to set apart the last Thursday in April next, as a day of fasting, humiliation and prayer, that our supplications may then ascend to the throne of the Ruler of the Universe, beseeching Him that he would to diffuse a spirit of universal reformation among all ranks and degrees of our citizens; and make us holy, that so we may be a happy people; that it would please Him to impart wisdom, integrity and unanimity to our counselors; to bless and prosper the reign of our illustrious ally, and give success to his arms employed in the defence of the rights of human nature; that He would smile upon our military arrangements by land and sea; administer comfort and consolation to our prisoners in a cruel captivity; that he would protect the health and life of our Commander in Chief; give grant us victory over our enemies; establish peace in all our borders, and give happiness to all our inhabitants; that he would prosper the labor of husbandman, making the earth yield its increase in abundance, and give a proper season for the in gathering of the fruits thereof; that He would grant success to all engaged in lawful trade and commerce, and take under his guardianship all schools and seminaries of learning, and make them nurseries of virtue and piety; that He would incline the hearts of all men to peace, and fill them with universal charity and benevolence, and that the religion of our Divine Redeemer, with all its benign influences, may cover the earth as the waters cover the seas.

Nov. 28, 1782

On the report of a committee, consisting of Mr. [John] Witherspoon, Mr. [Joseph] Montgomery and Mr.[Hugh] Williamson, appointed to prepare a recommendation to the states, setting apart a day of thanksgiving and prayer, Congress agreed to the following act:

It being the indispensable duty of all nations, not only to offer up their supplications to Almighty God, the giver of all good, for his gracious assistance in general, and especially for great and signal interpositions of his Providence in their behalf; therefore the United States in Congress assembled, taking into their consideration the many instances of divine goodness to these states, in the course of the important conflict in which they have been so long engaged; and drawing to a close, particularly the harmony of the public councils, which is so necessary to the success of the public cause; the perfect union and good understanding which has hitherto subsisted between them and their allies, notwithstanding the artful and unwearied attempts of the common enemy to sow dissension between them divide them; the success of the arms of the United States and those of their allies, and the acknowledgement of their independence by another European power, whose friendship and commerce must be of great and lasting advantage to these states; and the success of their arms and those of their allies in different parts do hereby recommend it to the inhabitants of these states in general, to observe, and recommend it to the executives of request the several states to interpose their authority in appointing and requiring commanding the observation of the last Thursday, in the 28th day of November next, as a day of solemn thanksgiving to God for all his mercies: and they do further recommend to all ranks, to testify their gratitude to God for his goodness, by a cheerful obedience to his laws, and by promoting, each in his station, and by his influence, the practice of true and undefiled religion, which is the great foundation of public prosperity and national happiness. Given, &c.

General Observations About the Days of Prayer

As one reads the different proclamations of these days of prayer and fasting, a pattern can be seen. With some variation, here is the pattern:

- We confess our sins and the need to get our lives right with God (through the merits of Jesus Christ)
- God help us in our present situation.
- Guide our rulers with wisdom.
- Guide our military forces.
- Bless the manufacturers of our country.
- Bless the husbandmen (farmers) with their crops.
- Bless the schools to be places of virtue, piety and true knowledge.
- Bless the cause of Christianity to spread over the whole world.

If you would like a recipe to fix our nation's ills, this looks like a great place to start. We do need to get our lives right with God. Through the merits of Jesus Christ would be difficult with the multicultural stress. We can stress the merits of Jesus Christ through many cultures. Jesus wants all nations to come to Him. His last words to his disciples in Matthew 28:19-20 were to make disciples of all nations.

We could use His help in our present situation. Our rulers surely need His wisdom. Our military surely needs His guidance. Our manufacturers surely need His blessing. The farmers stand in need of His blessing. Our schools need to be places of virtue, piety and true knowledge. We could be used of God to spread His light to the whole world. How is the light that comes out of the City on the Hill, is it shining brightly or is it dim?

STATE CONSTITUTIONS

Georgia

"We the people of Georgia, relying upon protection and guidance of Almighty God, do ordain and establish this Constitution." 1777

"VI. ...The representatives shall be chosen out of the residents of each county... and they shall be of the protestant religion, and of the age of twenty one years."

'XIV. Every person entitled to one vote shall take the following oath or affirmation, if required viz.

'I, A.B. do voluntarily and solemnly swear, or affirm, as the case may be, that I do allegiance to this state and will support the constitution thereof...So help me God."

South Carolina

"No person shall be eligible to sit in the house of representatives unless he be of the Protestant religion." March 19, 1778

"XXXVII...The Christian Protestant religion shall be deemed and is hereby constituted and declared to be, the established religion of this State. That all denominations of Christian Protestants in this State, demeaning themselves peaceably and faithfully, shall enjoy equal religious and civil privileges."

Every Christian group had to qualify for five basic points:

1. That there is one eternal God, and a future state of rewards and punishments.
2. That God is publicly to be worshipped.
3. That the Christian religion is the true religion.
4. That the holy scriptures of the Old and New Testaments are of divine inspiration, and are the rule of faith and practice.
5. That it is lawful and the duty of every man being thereunto called by those that govern, to bear witness to the truth."

North Carolina

"XXXII.(5) That no person, who shall deny the being of God or the truth of the Protestant religion, or the divine authority either of the Old or New Testaments, or who shall hold religious principles incompatible with the freedom and safety of the State, shall be capable of holding any office or place of trust or profit in the civil department within the State." North Carolina Constitution, Dec. 18, 1776

Virginia

Virginia Bill of Rights, June 12, 1776

"Article XVI That Religion, or the Duty which we owe our Creator, and the Manner or discharging it, can be directed only by Reason and Convictions, not by Force or Violence; and therefore all Men are equally entitled to the free exercise of Religion, according to the Dictates of Conscience; and that it is the mutual Duty of all to practice Christian Forbearance, Love and Charity towards each other."

Virginia Statute of Religious Liberty, Jan. 16, 1786

"Well aware that Almighty God hath created the mind free; that all attempts to influence it by temporal punishments or burdens, or by civil incapacitations...are a departure from the plan of the Holy Author of our religion."

Maryland

<u>Constitution of the State of Maryland</u>, August 14, 1776
"We, the people of the state of Maryland, grateful to Almighty God for our civil and religious liberty…"

"Article XXXV That no other test or qualification ought to be required, on admission to any office of trust or profit, than such oath of support and fidelity to this State and such oath of office, as shall be directed by this Convention, or the Legislature of this State, and a declaration of a belief in the Christian religion."

"Article XXXVI That the manner of administering an oath to any person, ought to be such, as those of the religious persuasion, profession, or denomination, of which such person is one, generally esteem to most effectual confirmation, by the attestation of the Divine Being."

"That, as it is the duty of every man to worship God is such a manner as he thinks most acceptable to him; all persons professing the Christian religion, are equally entitled to protection in their religious liberty;

"wherefore no person ought by any law to be molested… on account of his religious practice; unless, under the color [pretense] of religion, any man shall infringe the laws of morality.. yet the Legislature may, in their discretion, lay a general and equal tax, for the support of the Christian religion." [changed in 1851]

Delaware

<u>Constitution of the State of Delaware</u>, Sept. 21, 1776
"Article XXII. Every person who shall be chosen a member of either house, or appointed to any office of trust, before taking his seat, or entering upon the execution of his office, shall take the following oath, or affirmation, if conscientiously scrupulous of taking an oath, to wit:

"I, A.B. will bear true allegiance to the Delaware State, submit to its constitution and laws, and do no act wittingly whereby the freedom thereof may be prejudiced.

And also make and subscribe the following declaration, to wit:

"I, A.B. do profess faith in God the Father, and in Jesus Christ His only Son, and in the Holy Ghost, one God, blessed for evermore; and I do acknowledge the holy scriptures of the Old and New Testament to be given by divine inspiration."

New Jersey

New Jersey Constitution, July 2, 1776, XVIII

That no person shall ever, within this Colony, be deprived of the inestimable privilege of worshipping Almighty God in a manner, agreeable to the dictates of his own conscience; nor, under any presence whatever, be compelled to attend any place of worship, contrary to his own faith and judgment; nor shall any person, within this Colony, ever be obliged to pay tithes, taxes or any other rates, for the purpose of building or repairing any other church or churches, place or places of worship, or for the maintenance of any minister or ministry, contrary to what he believes to be right, or has deliberately or voluntarily engaged himself to perform.

New Jersey XIX

That there shall be no establishment of any one religious sect in this Province, in preference to another; and that no Protestant inhabitant of this Colony shall be denied the enjoyment of any civil right, merely on account of his religious principles; but that all persons, professing a belief in the faith of any Protestant sect who shall demean themselves peaceably under the government, as hereby established, shall be capable of being elected into any office of profit or trust, or being a member of either branch of the Legislature, and shall fully and freely enjoy every privilege and immunity, enjoyed by others their fellow subjects.

Pennsylvania

Pennsylvania Constitution, Sept. 28, 1776, II

"That all men have a natural and unalienable right to worship Almighty God according to the dictates of their own consciences and understanding: And that no man ought or of right can be compelled to attend any religious worship, or erect or support any place of worship, or maintain any ministry, contrary to, or against his own free will and consent: Nor can any man, who acknowledges the being of a God, be justly deprived or abridged of any civil right as a citizen, on account of his religious sentiments or peculiar mode of religious worship: And that no authority can or ought to be vested in, or assumed by any power whatever, that shall in any case interfere with, or in any manner control, the right of conscience in the free exercise of religious worship."

Section 10. "...And each member, before he takes his seat, shall make and subscribe the following declaration, viz:

I do believe in one God, the creator and governor of the universe, the rewarder of the good and the punisher of the wicked. And I do acknowledge the Scriptures of the Old and New Testament to be given by Divine inspiration.

And no further or religious test shall ever hereafter be required of any civil officer or magistrate in this State."

New York

Constitution of the State of New York, 1777

"The free exercise and enjoyment of religious profession and worship, without discrimination or preference, shall forever hereafter be allowed, within this State, to all mankind: Provided, that the liberty of conscience, hereby granted, shall not be construed as to excuse acts of licentiousness."

Connecticut

Constitution of the State of Connecticut

"The people of this State ...by the Providence of God...hath the sole and exclusive right of governing themselves as a free, sovereign, and independent State...and forasmuch as the free fruition of such liberties and privileges as humanity, civility and Christianity call for, as is due to every man in his place and proportion...hath ever been, and will be the tranquility and stability of Churches and

Commonwealth; and the denial thereof, the disturbances, if not the ruin of both."

Rhode Island, 1842

"We, the people of the State of Rhode Island and Providence Plantations, grateful to Almighty God for the civil and religious liberty which He hath so long permitted us to enjoy, and looking to Him for a blessing upon our endeavors to secure and transmit the same unimpaired to succeeding generations, do ordain and establish this constitution of Government."

New Hampshire

Constitution of the State of New Hampshire, 1784

Part One, Article I, Section V. "Every individual has a natural and unalienable right to worship God according to the dictates of his own conscience, and reason"

Article I, Section VI. "And every denomination of Christians demeaning themselves quietly, and as good citizens of the state, shall be equally under the protection of the laws. And no subordination of any one sect of denomination to another, shall ever be established by law."

Massachusetts

Constitution of the State of Massachusetts, 1780

"We, therefore, the people of Massachusetts, acknowledging, with grateful hearts, the goodness of the great Legislator of the universe, in affording us, in the course of his providence [an opportunity to form a compact];...and devoutly imploring His direction in so interesting a design,...[establish this Constitution].

"The governor shall be chosen annually; and no person shall be eligible to this office, unless, at the same time of his election... he shall declare himself to be of the Christian religion."

Chapter VI, Article I [All person elected to State office or to the Legislature must] make and subscribe the following declaration, viz. "I _____, do declare, that I believe the Christian religion, and have firm persuasion of its truth."

Part I, Article II "It is the right, as well as the duty, of all men in society, publicly, and at stated seasons, to worship the Supreme Being, the Great Creator and Preserver of the Universe. And no subject shall be hurt, molested, or restrained, in his person, liberty or estate, for worshipping God in the manner and seasons, most agreeable to the dictates of his own conscience."

Part I, Article III, "And every denomination of Christians, demeaning themselves peaceably, and as good subjects of the commonwealth, shall be equally under the protection of the law: and no subordination of any sect or denomination to another shall ever be established by law."

God's Providential Care in the War for Independence

This section will attempt to show seven instances of how people at the time of the founding of the nation attested the birth of the country to God's Providence. Remember Jay's words: **"a proper history of the United States would develop the great plan of Providence...The historian, in the course of the work, is never to lose sight of that great plan."**

There are probably many more instances of God's hand during the period of the War for Independence. The following are gleaned from <u>America's Providential History</u> by Stephen McDowell and Mark Beliles and <u>The Light and the Glory</u> by Peter Marshall and David Manuel

<u>The Sacrifice of Delaware and Maryland
at the Battle of Brooklyn</u>

The Declaration of Independence was signed July 2/4, 1776. The British sent their reply at the battle of Brooklyn. During the first part of July, 1776 most of the Continental Congress was meeting in Philadelphia. The Declaration of Independence was written during that time period. John Jay and others of the New York delegation were in New York. They had to deal with the pressing problem of 82 British ships of the line off the shores of New York City.

The British army had already engaged the American militia in 1775 in the Boston region (Lexington and Concord). The British military leadership decided to go for New York. If they could capture New York and take the Hudson River, they could sever the colonies into two parts and win the war. In August they struck and landed British marines (similar to what was seen at Normandy in World War II). The American troops were outnumbered and easily defeated.

On August 22, the British landed with 15,000 troops. The American forces under George Washington (General Israel Putnam of Bunker Hill fame was in charge of the Brooklyn section) only numbered 8,000. The British added to their superiority by landing about 5,000 Hessians. At the time of the battle, British forces numbered over 30,000. Severely outnumbered and out-trained, the Americans were no match for the British. It could have been all over for the American cause at this point. The Maryland and Delaware battalions gave up their lives so that the rest of the army could retreat.

With 400 Marylanders against a force of 2,000 British (and they were being reinforced in addition to the 2,000) the leaders Sterling and Gist made a daring decision. The Marylanders charged into the rain of British fire. Sterling led six charges into swelling British reinforcements and Cornwallis' light cannon. The Marylanders' sacrificial bravery allowed the rest of the Continentals in the field to escape across the Gowanus Creek and live to fight another day. Maryland lost 256 men and Delaware lost 261 men on that day.

Because of the bravery of the Maryland forces, Washington allowed the Maryland flag to be flown at the same height as the United States flag (however, it should never be of a bigger size than the United States flag).

When Washington was informed of (and saw) the sacrifice of the Maryland and Delaware groups, he wrung his hands and said: "Good God, what brave fellows I must this day lose!" The British General Howe did not follow up the attack immediately and waited a few days. Washington called on the Marbleheaders under John Glover and the 27th Massachusetts to lead a retreat by boat across the East River. They would join up with the main body of the American forces under Henry Knox at the foot of Manhattan Island. A divine fog set in so that the American forces could retreat. If there had been a storm, circumstances would have been different. The Americans would not have been able to take their heavy guns across because the small boats would have sunk with heavy wake. If the weather had been clear, the British ships would have seen them and had a shooting gallery massacre.

On August 29 the weather was threatening and the British held off any attack. A hard rain fell in the late afternoon. The rain was a northeast rain that prevented the British from entering the East River. At this point Washington came up with the plan to evacuate by boats. After midnight, the wind died away. All night long the Marbleheaders (led by Colonel John Glover from Massachusetts) and the 27th Massachusetts men rowed men to the other shore quietly, dipping their paddles with the least noise possible. When dawn came, there were still many Americans in the trenches. An eyewitness account (Major Ben Tallmadge) relates: "a very dense fog began to rise [out of the ground and off the river], and it seemed to settle in a peculiar manner over both encampments. I recollect this peculiar providential occurrence perfectly well, and so very dense was the atmosphere that I could scarcely discern a man at six yards distance." The fog remained until the last boat, with Washington in it, left. When it lifted, the shocked British ran to the shore and fired their guns at them, but the Americans were out of range. The only people captured were some petty thieves who were trying to rummage through the Continental Army's leftovers. God's Providence was looking over our weak army and allowed us to keep fighting another day. The evacuation on the 29th and 30th was also made possible by the sacrifice by the brave Delaware and Maryland battalions on the 27th who sacrificed their lives so that the struggle could go on.

Most battlefields are left alone in a sort of sacred remembrance to those who died on the field. People will go out and see Gettysburg, Manassas, Antietam, Valley Forge, Yorktown, etc. and remember their sacrifice. Brooklyn is not in the American psyche as a place of remembrance, but it should be. The city grew up all around the battleground and streets and buildings mark the site now. One has to work hard to visualize the scene nowadays. There is a monument to the Maryland and Delaware battalions that fought there. Further reading on the subject can be found in a book entitled "The Battle of Brooklyn, 1776" by John J. Gallagher.

Washington Crossing the Delaware

At the end of the month, all the enlistments were up. At the beginning of the new year, most of the men's duty would be over and few had re-enlisted. The morale of the troops was low. Washington decided to cross over the Delaware River in a bold move to surprise the Hessian troops on December 26. Washington expected that they would have been drinking heavily on Christmas day and would be sleeping in that morning. Christmas day for the American troops was a rough one. A violent snow and hail storm came up. Visibility was near zero and the Hessian sentries sought cover. The storm worked in our favor. The crossing was bitter cold but it made the Hessians stay inside. When our troops finally arrived after marching in the night and morning, they took about 1000 prisoners in only 45 minutes of fighting. Only 6 Americans were wounded in the battle (one of whom was James Monroe). Two Americans froze to death on the march before they got there. General Henry Knox described the battle: "The hurry, fright and confusion of the enemy was not unlike that which will be when the last trump will sound."

Two days before Washington's Crossing of the Delaware, John Jay gave an address to the New York Assembly which had asked him to write something to lift the morale of the people of New York. "The Address of the Convention of the Representatives of the State of New York" contained at least 33 mentions of God and having faith in God. It was translated into German and sent to the people at government expense to encourage them during this difficult time.

Saratoga

General Burgoyne led about 7,000 British troops along with Germans, Loyalists and Indians from Canada in June 1777. His plan was to go south from Quebec and capture Albany, New York and join up with Colonel St. Leger's forces from the west on the Mohawk River and General Howe coming north from New York In July, 1777

1776 Faith

he captured Fort Ticonderoga after moving 20 miles through very tough terrain in 26 days. St. Leger's camp heard a rumor that Benedict Arnold was coming up the Mohawk River after him with 3,500 men (actually it was only 1,000) and the Tories and Indians dispersed. In August, part of his army was defeated near Bennington, Vermont. A New Hampshire army funded by John Langdon and commanded by General John Stark put 900 German soldiers under Burgoyne out of the war and only 70 Americans lost their lives. Fighting went on for a month but Burgoyne finally surrendered.

We lost the battle of Brandywine (Pennsylvania) in September 1777 where 1200 Americans lost their lives. On October 17, 1777 our side won at Saratoga. The British General Howe was supposed to have marched north to join Burgoyne's men at Saratoga. In his haste to leave for London for a holiday, Lord North forgot to sign the dispatch to General Burgoyne. Also, contrary winds kept British delayed at sea for 3 months. God worked in our favor again. A Day of Thanksgiving and Praise to God was set apart for December 18, 1777 by the Continental Congress as a way to thank God for looking over the American cause. That is not my editorializing, that was what the Continental Congress decided was appropriate.

After so many defeats, the battle at Saratoga was a turning point. It convinced France that the American cause was a worthy cause and not a hopeless one.

Valley Forge

In the winter of 1777-78, Valley Forge was another ordeal for the men to struggle through. What sustained Washington through the trying winter? During most of January and February, there were constantly more than 4,000 soldiers who were unfit for duty. Washington would seek a solitary place and bear his burden to God. How did God answer? Listen to this story:

> "One foggy morning the soldiers noticed the Schuykill River seemed to be boiling. The disturbance was caused by thousands and thousands of shad which were making their way upstream in an unusually early migration. With pitchforks

and shovels, the men plunged into the water, throwing the fish onto the banks. Lee's dragoons rode their horses into the streams to keep the shad from swimming out of reach. Suddenly and wonderfully, there was plenty of food for the army."

France agreed to join in an alliance with us that winter. At Valley Forge on May 5, 1778, Washington issued the following orders:

"It having pleased the Almighty Ruler of the Universe propitiously to defend the cause of the United American States, and finally by raising up a powerful friend among the Princes of the earth, to establish our Liberty and Independence upon a lasting foundation; it becomes us to set apart a day for gratefully acknowledging the Divine Goodness, and celebrating the event, which we owe to His benign interposition."

Benedict Arnold's Betrayal

Another example of God's hand on our nation was the finding out of the treason of Benedict Arnold. He was in charge of West Point. In today's time, we all think of the United States Military Academy where the army trains its leaders. During our fight for independence, West Point held a very strategic point. No ships could pass this point without being hit by gunfire. If Great Britain could gain this spot, they could control the Hudson River, split the country in two and conquer it. However, be sure your sins will find you out! Arnold's treason was!

On September 26, 1780, General Washington sent the following message to his troops (delivered by General Greene):

"Treason of the blackest dye was yesterday discovered! General Arnold who commanded at West Point, lost to every sentiment of honor, of public and private obligation, was about to deliver up that important Post into the hands of the enemy. Such an event must have been given the American cause a deadly wound if not a fatal stab. Happily the treason has been timely discovered to prevent the fatal misfortune. The Providential train of circumstances which led to it affords the most convincing proof that the liberties of America are the object of Divine Providence."

The Continental Congress, in response to the news, on the 18th of October, 1780 made a resolution and set apart December 7, 1780 as a day of thanksgiving and prayer. It is interesting to note that the Continental Congress in this declaration wanted to "cause the knowledge of Christianity to spread over all the earth."

The Retreat From the Battle of Cowpens

The retreat from the battle of Cowpens is another example of God's hand upon us. Our army in the south was outnumbered but the Americans beat the British at Cowpens on January 17, 1781. Again, our strategy was hit and run. This battle is depicted in "The Patriot." The Americans utilized militia to fire at the British lines then retreated and the British followed them thinking this would be an easy killing. The Continental Army under Nathaniel Greene was waiting for the British and won the battle.

After the defeat, General Cornwallis tried to cut off the retreat of the American army. He reached the Catawba River just two hours after General Morgan (the American leader) had crossed. Cornwallis waited until morning to cross. During the night a storm came up and filled the river which delayed his troops. Two more times in the next 10 days Cornwallis almost had the Americans. On February 3, he reached the Yadkin River in North Carolina just as the Americans were landing on the eastern slopes. Before he could cross, a sudden flood cut off the British troops again! On February 13, the Americans reached the Dan River. This would lead them to friendly Virginia territory. The Americans crossed over and a few hours later, guess what happened- the waters would not let the British cross over. Three times the American army could relate to Israel's experience of crossing the Red Sea while Pharaoh's army was bearing down on them. Three times God granted deliverance. This set of circum-

stances drove Cornwallis to the sea where he would meet his final defeat at Yorktown.
(Peter Marshall, Jr. speech at ASCI Conference, Jan. 1998)

Surrender of Cornwallis at Yorktown

Yorktown gives us another example of God's provision for the American cause. In October of 1781, General Cornwallis had his troops at Yorktown in Virginia. During the same time, General Washington marched his troops from New York to Yorktown. Unknown to either side, the French fleet beat the British fleet off Cape Henry. The British fleet could not give Cornwallis the reinforcements he needed. The combined American and French forces were besieging Yorktown. Cornwallis tried to retreat across the York River to Gloucester. At 10 o'clock on the night of October 17, he loaded 16 large boats with troops and set off for Gloucester. A storm came up and drove all the boats down the river. Cornwallis was unable to complete his retreat. His force was divided when the Americans batteries opened fire the next morning. Later that day he surrendered to General Washington.

When the Continental Congress heard the news, they went to a church at 2:00 to give thanks to God. When Washington informed his troops, he invited them to a divine service the next day. He recommended "that the troops not on duty should universally attend with that seriousness of deportment and gratitude of heart which the recognition of such reiterated and astonishing interpositions of Providence demand of us."

George Whitefield   Jonathan Edwards   Samuel Davies

The Great Awakening

This book cannot ignore the impact of the Great Awakening, because it laid the foundation for the worldview of the Founders. New England from its inception, had religion (specifically Christianity) as the engine of life. The Pilgrims came in 1620 and the Puritans followed. Pilgrims believed that they should <u>come out of</u> the organized church. The Puritans were also believers but they differed in that they <u>stayed in</u> the organized church. Both groups desired to be used of God to bring the organized church back to being faithful to God and the Bible. John Winthrop's phrase "City on a Hill" epitomized the desire of early New Englanders.

After the passing of one hundred years, the spiritual fervor and passion had declined. People were more concerned about material prosperity than spiritual matters. Theodore Frelinghuysen, a Dutch Reformed minister in New Jersey was shocked at the spiritual deadness in the churches at that time (1720s). Gilbert Tennant was used of God in New Jersey through Frelinghuysen's influence. Tennant wrote <u>On the Dangers of an Unconverted Ministry</u>. He quoted Matthew 15:14 "For if the blind lead the blind, will they not both fall into the ditch?" Ministers of the Gospel then as well as now need to be converted wholly to Christ before they can truly minister.

Jonathan Edwards as a child struggled with the sovereignty of God. He had a tremendous intellect that is still highly respected today. Before he was thirteen years old, he had studied in depth Greek, Hebrew and Latin. The text of I Timothy 1:7 changed him:

"Now unto the King eternal, immortal, invisible, the only wise God, be honor and glory forever and ever, Amen." That verse is well worth meditating on if it impacted Edwards so well. Edwards became pastor of his grandfather's church in Northampton, Massachusetts in 1729. Revival started in 1735. Jonathan wrote <u>A Faithful Narrative of the Suprising Work of God in 1737</u>. This book was widely circulated in America and England.

George Whitefield was influenced by Edwards' book and came to America and starting preaching in 1740. If your history textbook happens to mention Whitefield (most public high schools God [or whatever] forbid would not mention him), take careful note to see how the book portrays him. There are some good pictures of Whitefield available but I have noticed quite a few books show him as a cross-eyed buffoon. He appealed across denominational lines. Baptists, Methodists (followers of John Wesley), Presbyterians, Dutch Reformed and some Catholics listened to Whitefield. He traveled through the colonies seven times and died in 1770.

He possessed great oratorical skills and spoke to crowds as large as 10,000. Franklin built a hall specifically for Whitefield to preach. A lesson to learn from comparing Whitefield to Wesley, is that Whitefield was a better speaker but Wesley put much of his energy into organizing and discipling his followers.

Samuel Davies was greatly used by God in Virginia as a conduit for revival there. Having started his ministry in 1745 and then losing his young wife and son in 1747, Davies decided to go into overdrive and be spent for God's kingdom. He later became president of Princeton briefly. On New Year's Day, 1761 he preached "This Year You Shall Die" and died in February. Did any signers of the Declaration happen to be attending at that time? Benjamin Rush was as well as other people in the vanguard of the new group of leaders were there at that time.

What do these preachers and the Great Awakening have to do with the Founding Fathers? The Founders grew up in a country that was permeated with the Christian worldview. Let's step back a moment and see how this relates to the Founders. Elias Boudinot (the President of the Continental Congress when the Treaty of Paris was signed) was baptized by George Whitefield. Whitefield was a personal friend of Ben Franklin. Roger Sherman was a deacon under Jonathan Edwards. Benjamin Rush was a student of Samuel Davies at Princeton. Samuel Johnson was important as an Anglican in the Great Awakening. He tutored Jonathan Edwards at Yale and later became the president of King's College in New York and was there while John Jay was a student.

Keep in mind that 10 of the Signers were sons of ministers: Philip Livingston, Francis Lewis, George Taylor, George Ross, Samuel Chase, John Witherspoon, John Hancock, Robert Treat Paine, William Williams and William Hooper. Quite a few also had grandfathers that were ministers. Quite a few had mothers who were the daughters of ministers. Quite a few had wives that were daughters of ministers. George Wythe was a descendant of the Bishop of London.

For all of you that maintain that they were all deists and atheists, just give it up. It is a heart problem more than an intellectual one. In the parable of the rich man and Lazarus, the rich man asked Abraham to send someone to warn his five brothers to stay away from hell. Abraham told him: "If they do not listen to Moses and the Prophets, they will not be convinced even if someone rises from the dead." For many people, it is a heart issue. "We will not have this man Jesus to rule over us. We want to run our own lives without God." I implore you to follow the example of these imperfect sinners who signed the Declaration and tried to live a life for God and leave something for their posterity. The offer of eternal life is offered to you, reader. Do you desire this life in Christ or do you wish to turn your back? Witherspoon, Sherman, Jay, Williams, Rush, Hopkinson, and company are interested in your decision. They implore you to come to their Heavenly Father

Johann Sebastian Bach   Isaac Watts   John Newton   George Frideric Handel

Music During the American Revolution

When one searches for music of the American Revolutionary era, it becomes self evident that the people doing the editing cut out the religious music. You will probably see CDs with Yankee Doodle, and all the secular songs you would ever want. Those songs are fine- it's the editing out of the religious songs that I object to. It's the same old story when you go to most historical site bookstores or gift shops. Many steps are taken to insure that the store has been sanitized from all things Christian. Do you think that these people who have impressed us so deeply with their Christian worldview in their writings, turned on some switch and said: "We only do secular music"? The people that said "No king but King Jesus" also sung about Him. What Christian songs did they sing? If all that you have been fed are shallow choruses repeated twenty times, get ready for some depth.

Let's start with Rev. James Caldwell, a Presbyterian minister. He was also a chaplain for the Continental Army. He pastured a church near Elizabethtown, New Jersey. Among his church members was Elias Boudinot (later President of the Continental Congress as well as President of the American Bible Society). Rev. Caldwell came to service on Sundays with his pistol. The church was burnt to the ground in January 1780 by a Tory sympathizer. In June of that same year British came for him and others. When Rev. Caldwell met up with the local militia in Springfield, they were defeating the British but were running out of paper wadding. Paper wadding was important because it helped soldiers know how much gunpowder to load (if you loaded too much you could kill yourself instead of the enemy). Caldwell ordered the men back to the local Presbyterian church where he used the hymnals as paper wadding. As he was ripping up paper, he was encouraging the troops by saying: "Give 'em Watts boys!" He found out that day that the British had shot his wife in the head. Caldwell was shot in the next year. He and his wife left behind nine children, whom others adopted (Lafayette adopted one of the children).

People had Bibles and hymnals and were familiar with Isaac Watts' hymns. Handel's Messiah was first played in 1741 and was first played in 1770 in New York. John Adams heard it performed when he was in London after the War for Independence.

Some readers may be totally unfamiliar with hymns. As a sampler, check out the words of some of these hymns by Isaac Watts. He wrote at least 600 hymns and started English hymnody. He put all 150 Psalms to music (as did Francis Hopkinson, a signer of the Declaration of Independence from New Jersey).

Joy to the World

Joy to the world! The Lord is come; Let earth receive her King.
Let every heart prepare Him room, And heaven and nature sing.

Joy to the world! The Savior reigns; Let men their songs employ.
While fields and floods, rocks hills and plains, Repeat the sounding joy.

No more let sin or sorrow grow; Nor thorns infest the ground.
He comes to make His blessings flow, Far as the curse is found.

He rules the world with truth and grace And makes the nations prove
The glories of His righteousness And wonders of His love.

Alas! And Did My Savior Bleed?

Alas! And did my Savior bleed And did my Sov'reign die?
Would He devote that sacred head For such a worm as I?

Was it for sins that I have done He suffered on the tree?
Amazing pity! Grace unknown! And love beyond degree!

Well might the sun in darkness hide And shut His glories in,
When Christ, the great Redeemer, died For man the creature's sin.

But drops of grief can ne'er repay The debt of love I owe;
Here, Lord, I give myself away- Tis all that I can do.

When I Survey the Wondrous Cross

When I survey the wondrous cross On which the Prince of Glory died, My richest gain I count but loss And pour contempt on all my pride.

Forbid it Lord, that I should boast, Save in the death of Christ my God;
All the vain things that charm me most- I sacrifice them to His blood.
See, from His head, His hands, His feet, Sorrow and love flow mingled down
Did e'er such love and sorrow meet, Or thorns compose so rich a crown?

Were the whole realm of nature mine, That were a present far too small:
Love so amazing, so divine, Demands my soul, my life, my all.

Jesus Shall Reign

Jesus shall reign where'er the sun Does its successive journeys run;
His kingdom spread from shore to shore, Till moons shall wax and wane no more.

To Him shall endless prayer be made, And endless praises crown His head.
His name like sweet perfume shall rise With every morning sacrifice.

People and realms of every tongue Dwell on His love with sweetest song.
And infant voices shall proclaim Their early blessings on His name.

Let every creature rise and bring His grateful honors to our King;
Angels descend with songs again, And earth repeat the loud "Amen!"

O God Our Help In Ages Past

O God, our Help in ages past, Our Hope for years to come,
Our shelter from the stormy blast, And our eternal Home!

Under the shelter of Thy throne, Still may we dwell secure;
Sufficient is Thine arm alone, And our defense is sure.

Before the hills in order stood, Or earth received her frame,
From everlasting Thou art God, To endless years the same.

A thousand ages in Thy signt Are like an evening gone;
Short as the watch that ends the night Before the rising sun.
Time, like an ever-rolling stream, Bears all its sons away;
They fly, forgotten, as a dream Dies at the o-p'ning day.

O God our Help in ages past, Our Hope for years to come,
Be Thou our Guide while life shall last, And our eternal Home.

Besides Isaac Watts' hymns, there are quite a few psalter collections. The New England Version of the Psalms was printed in 1715. The Scottish Psalter had been around since 1615. Charles Wesley had many hymns out during this time. Phillip Doddridge's Hymns came out in 1755. Witt's Psalmodia Sacra was available.

Take note of the dates of the following musicians, hymn writers, ministers and political people of the era:

George Washington (1732-1799)
John Jay (1745-1829)
Thomas Jefferson (1746-1826)
Benjamin Franklin (1706- 1790)
Isaac Watts (1674-1748)
Johann Sebastian Bach (1685-1750)
George Frederick Handel (1685-1759)
John Newton (1725-1807)
Wolfgang Amadeus Mozart (1756- 1791)
John Wesley (1703-1791)
George Whitefield (1714-1770)
Jonathan Edwards (1703-1758)
Gilbert Tennant (1703-1764)

America's Early Christian Colleges

The college life of the Founding Fathers was vastly different from that of today. Of the first 108 colleges in the United States, 106 were founded on the Christian faith. It is difficult for many students living today to even envision studying at a college where the day and the class started with prayer. Take the Founder's Challenge concerning the Christian history of colleges and you might be surprised at what they were like at the beginning. Again, be ready to dig; don't take the first superficial answer as a clue to stop asking questions. Some things are intentionally hidden, other aspects are scoffed at as being outdated and naïve. We, of course, know better now.

Harvard was founded in 1638. Rev. John Harvard gave half of his property and his entire library to start this Congregational institution. In the Old Deluder Satan Act of 1647 it was ordered that every township containing 50 families or householders should set up a school in which children might be taught to read and write, and that every township containing 100 families or householders should set up a school in which boys might be fitted for entering Harvard College. The motto of Harvard was: "For Christ and the Church." (Seal: "Christo et Ecclesia"). Check out these rules: "Let every Student be plainly instructed, and earnestly pressed to consider well, the maine end of his life and studies is, to know God and Jesus Christ which is eternal life, (John 17:3), and therefore to lay Christ in the bottome, as the only foundation of all sound knowledge and Learning."

Yale was established in 1701 "for the liberal and religious education of suitable youth...to propagate in this wilderness, the blessed reformed Protestant religion..." "Seeing God is the giver of all wisdom, every scholar, besides private or secret prayer, where all we are bound to ask wisdom, shall be present morning and evening at public prayer in the hall at the accustomed hour..."

Princeton was founded by Presbyterians in 1746. It had Samuel Davies and Rev. John Witherspoon, among others as its president during the formative years for those in the American Revolution. The first president of Princeton, Jonathan Dickinson said the following about the direction of Princeton: "Cursed be all learning that is contrary to the cross of Christ." Princeton's motto was: "Under God's Power She Flourishes."

Rutgers (Queen's College) was founded in 1766 by Rev. Theodore Frelinghuysen, Dutch Reformed minister. Its purpose was "for the education of youth in the learned languages, liberal and useful arts and sciences, and especially in divinity, preparing them for the ministry and other good offices." Rutgers' motto was: "Son of Righteousness, Shine upon the West also."

King's College/Columbia University was established in 1754. Samuel Johnson, one of the Anglican ministers of the Great Awakening was president when John Jay was a student. While John Jay was a student there, morning and evening prayers were a part of the studies. William Samuel Johnson took over the college and you should read his address to the first graduating class from Columbia: "Remember, too that you are the redeemed of the Lord, that you are bought with a price, even the inestimable price of the precious blood of the Son of God." Do they still have those kinds of commencement speakers at Columbia?

William and Mary College was started in 1692 as a school for preparing ministers. Rev. James Blair was sent to establish "a certain Place of Universal Study, a perpetual College of Divinity, Philosophy, Languages, and the good arts and sciences." Upon completion of their work, the Divinity School prepared young men for ordination into the Church of England. The first 8 presidents were ministers including the last one, Bishop James Madison (not the fourth president, but a relative) from 1776-1812.

Most all the colleges had morning and evening prayers. The sad situation is that prayer has been taken off most campuses. If you are past college age, put these colleges and the colleges in your state on your prayer list. Ask God to send his Holy Spirit to awaken these schools that once honored Jesus Christ to welcome Him once again. If you are a student at one of these historically Christian schools, start a prayer group.

"Jesus shall reign where'er the sun Does its successive journeys run; His kingdom spread from shore to shore, Till moons shall wax and wane no more." Isaac Watts

David Barton, Original Intent. pp 81-84
William Federer, America's God and Country.

Bibliography

Barton, David. <u>Original Intent</u>. Aledo, Texas: Wallbuilder Press, 1996.

Barton, David. <u>The Bullet-Proof George Washington</u>. Aledo, Texas: Wallbuilder Press, 2003.

Barton, David. <u>Benjamin Rush: Signer of the Declaration of Independence</u>. Aledo, Texas: Wallbuilder Press, 1999.

Beliles, Mark and Stephen K. McDowell. <u>America's Providential History</u>. Charlottesville, Virginia: Providence Press, 1989.

Boyd, George Adams. <u>Elias Boudinot: Patriot and Statesman, 1740-1821</u>. New York: Greenwood Press, 1969 (reprinted from Princeton Univ. Press, 1952).

Bradford, M.E. <u>Founding Fathers: Brief Lives of the Framers of the United States Constitution</u>. 2nd edition. Lawrence, Kansas: University Press of Kansas, 1994.

Broadman, Roger Sherman. <u>Roger Sherman: Signer and Statesman</u>. New York: Da Capo Press, 1971(reprinted from Philadelphia: University of Pennsylvania Press, 1938).

Brown, Abram English. <u>John Hancock: His Book</u>. Boston: Lee and Shepherd Publishers, 1898.

Brown, Imogene. American Aristides: A Biography of George Wythe. Rutherford, New Jersey: Farleigh Dickinson University Press, 1981.

Candler, Allen D., ed., The Revolutionary Period of the State of Georgia. Vol. I & II, Atlanta: The Franklin-Turner Company, 1908.

Eidsmoe, John. The Christian Legal Adviser. Grand Rapids, Michigan: Baker Book House, 1984.

Eidsmoe, John. Christianity and the Constitution: The Faith of Our Founding Fathers. Grand Rapids, Michigan: Baker Book House, 1995.

Federer, William J. America's God and Country Encyclopedia of Quotations. Coppell, Texas: FAME Publishing, Inc., 1994.

Ford, Worthington Chauncey, editor. Journals of Continental Congress. v. 1-15, Sept. 5, 1774-Dec. 31, 1779 by Worthington Chauncey Ford.—v. 16-27, Jan. 1, 1780-Dec. 24, 1784 by Gaillard Hunt.—v. 28-31, Jan. 11, 1785-Dec. 31, 1786 by John C. Fitzpatrick.—v. 32-34, Jan. 17, 1787-March 2, 1789 by Roscoe R. Hill. U.S. Government Printing Office, http://memory.loc.gov/ammem/amlaw/lwjclink.html

Grant, George. The Patriot's Handbook. Nashville: Cumberland House Publishing, 1996.

Hakim, Joy. A History of US. New York: Oxford University Press, 1999. Vol. I-IV.

Hamilton, Alexander, James Madison and John Jay. The Federalist Papers. New York: Bantam Books, 1988. (first published in 1787-1788).

Jay, William. The Life of John Jay. Bridgewater, Virginia: American Foundation Publications, 1995 (reprinted from 1833 edition).

Johnston, Henry P. ed. The Correspondence and Public Papers of John Jay 1745-1826. New York: Da Capo Press, 1971. (republication in one volume of the four-volume edition published in New York between 1890 and 1893).

Kaye, Harvey J. Thomas Paine: Firebrand of the Revolution. New York: Oxford University Press, 2000.

Lee, Nell Moore. Patriot Above Profit: A Portrait of Thomas Nelson, Jr. Who Supported the American Revolution. Nashville, Tennessee: Rutledge Hill Press, 1988.

Lossing, Benson J. Lives of the Signers of the Declaration of Independence. New York: George F. Cooledge & Brother, 1858; reprinted by Wallbuilder Press, 1996.

Malone, Dumas. The Story of the Declaration of Independence. New York: Oxford University Press, 1954.

Marble, Anne Russell. "Francis Hopkinson," Heralds of American Literature. Chicago: The University of Chicago Press, 1907, pp.17-58.

Marshall, Peter and David Manuel. The Light and the Glory. Grand Rapids, Michigan: Fleming H. Revell Press, 1977.

McCullough, David. John Adams. New York: Simon & Schuster, 2001.

McDowell, Stephen and Mark Beliles. In God We Trust: Tour Guide. Charlottesville, Virginia: Providence Foundation, 1998.

Meade, Robert Douthat. *Patrick Henry: Patriot in the Making*. Philadelphia: J.B. Lippincott Co., 1957.

Millard, Catherine. *Great American Statesmen and Heroes*. Camp Hill, PA: Horizon Books, 1995.

Monaghan, Frank. *John Jay: Defender of Liberty*. New York: The Bobbs-Merrill Company, 1935. (reprinted AMS Press, Inc., New York, 1972).

Morris, Richard B. *John Jay: The Making of a Revolutionary*. New York: Harper & Row, Publishers, 1980.

Morris, Richard B. *John Jay: The Winning of the Peace*. New York: Harper and Row, Publishers, 1980.

Morris, Richard B. *John Jay: The Nation and the Court*. Boston: Boston University Press, 1967.

Morris, Richard B. *The Peacemakers*. New York: Harper and Row, Publishers, 1965.

Murray, Stuart. *American Revolution*. New York: Dorling-Kindersley Eyewitness Books, 2002.

Paine, Thomas. *Common Sense*. New York: Bantam Press, 2004.

Pellew, George. *John Jay*. Broomhall, Pennsylvania: Chelsea House Publishers, 1890 (reprinted 1997).

Powell, Phelan. *Revolutionary War Leaders: John Jay, First Chief Justice of the Supreme Court*. Philadelphia: Chelsea House Publishers, 2000.

Rose, Matthew. *John Witherspoon: An American Leader*. Washington, D.C.: Family Research Council, 1999.

Sheldon, Garrett Ward and Daniel L. Dreisbach. Religion and Political Culture in Jefferson's Virginia. Lanham, Maryland: Rowman & Littlefield, 2000.

Smith, Paul H. editor, Letters of the Continental Congress 1774-1789. Library of Congress, 1983, Vol. I-XXV. http://memory.loc.gov/ammem/amlaw/lwdglink.html

Stiverson, Gregory A. and Phoebe R. Jacobsen. William Paca: A Biography. Baltimore, Maryland: Historical Society, 1976.

Walton, Rus. One Nation Under God. Marlborough, New Hampshire: Plymouth Rock Foundation, 1993.

Wilson, Vincent, Jr. The Book of the Founding Fathers. Brookeville, Maryland: American History Research Associates, 1974.

Yates, Christopher S. Alexander Hamilton: How the Mighty are Redeemed. Washington, D.C.: Family Research Council, 2000.

Picture Credits

Cover: "The Continentals" draft drawing by Frank B Maier. Courtesy of my wife Jean and the Renshaw family. I particularly like the lack of faces in the background because it serves as a reminder that to many in our country the people and principles of the Founders is hidden or out of focus.

Breinigsville, PA USA
18 November 2009
227723BV00003B/2/P